D1429800

THE LAST STRAW

THE AUTOPSY OF THE LAST FILM IN THE STAR WARS FRANCHISE

JOHN C WRIGHT

Wisecraft

Copyright © 2019 by John C Wright

All rights reserved.

No part of this book may be reproduced in any form or by any electronic or mechanical means, including information storage and retrieval systems, without written permission from the author, except for the use of brief quotations in a book review.

CONTENTS

As I came through the desert thus it was,
As I came through the desert: Eyes of fire
Glared at me throbbing with a starved desire;
The hoarse and heavy and carnivorous breath
Was hot upon me from deep jaws of death;
Sharp claws, swift talons, fleshless fingers cold
Plucked at me from the bushes, tried to hold:
But I strode on austere;
No hope could have no fear.

— "The City of Dreadful Night"
by **Bysshe Vanolis**

STAR WARS ANONYMOUS

Hello, my name is John. I am a *Star Wars* addict. But with this new, twelve-step lobotomy-via-electroshock combined with savage groin kick therapy known as *Last Jedi*, I hope to be clean, sane, sober, and free from Star Wars for the rest of my natural life, and my next three reincarnations.

If anything can break an addiction to *Star Wars*, this can. *The Last Jedi* was the last straw.

It was the Last Film in the Franchise I will watch, and the Last Dime the Disney version of Star Wars will get out of me. I am not throwing away my cute R2D2 wastepaper basket, but I am not buying any new toy lightsabers either.

My sad story is no doubt the same as many a fans'.

I was young and impressionable when I first saw *Star Wars* in the theater (This is the flick you young whippersnappers call *A New Hope* or Episode IV).

The eye-dazzling special effects, the stirring John William's music, the unabashed and, yes, true-blue American sense of derring-do, adventure, heroism, romance, and chivalry shone like precious gold from every beloved line and frame of the film. Sure, it was Buck Rogers. It was rip-roaring space opera, heavy on the cornball and light on the science. But that was what won my undying affection.

Who cannot love a story of a spunky space princess fighting an evil space empire, aided by a freshly-scrubbed space farm boy who dreams of bigger things, the wise old space wizard, a lovable rogue with a heart of gold, his beloved jalopy (the fastest hunk of junk in the galaxy), his loyal pet Space Bigfoot, as well as a fussy robot butler, and a brave little Hoover vacuum cleaner? These are the most famous and most well-beloved characters in movies. To find their like, you have to go back to 1939's *Wizard of Oz*.

In those days, before streaming visuals, before Netflix, before Blockbuster, before VCRs, watching a film a second and third time in the theater, much less fifth or sixth, was an expensive proposition. But I was hooked. I vowed I would be a fan for life.

It is with tearful eye and aching heart that I here and now break, repudiate, and denounce that vow.

The prequels were lame, but my faith was only wounded, not killed; and when Disney got ahold of the most valuable intellectual property on Earth, I felt a new hope.

Surely Disney's people, who have been master story-tellers and filmmakers for generations, will be able to stick to the simple formula of the Buck Rogers Sci-Fi serial format, and tell a good tale. Space princess! Space farm boy! Lovable rogue! How can anyone mess that up? Had they not a ready-made deposit of Extended Universe comics, novels, and gaming materials with a rich background of tales and plots and story-elements ready to hand? It was an obscenely bloated cash cow of space, who gave green milk made of money.

The people sometimes called fanboys, but by the wise called loyal, lifelong, cash-heavy customers with disposable income, did not make undue demands. All they asked was not to be bored, not to have their intelligence insulted, not to have their beloved space fairytale of princesses and star-knights mocked and derided and deconstructed and turned into a political football.

All the filmmaker had to do was not suck. That was all.

Well, I saw *The Force Awakens*, and then saw *Rogue One*, and they were worse than lame. They sucked like hard vacuum. Hopes died. When *Last Jedi* hit the theaters, the once-blinding white-hot fires of love and loyalty of my fannish heart for the franchise had died to ashes so cold that I was utterly indifferent, utterly unconcerned.

I did not want to see the film. I was not curious. Everyone said *Last Jedi* was lame, except for those who said it sucked.

As it turns out, it did not suck. *Highlander II* sucked. *Plan Nine from Outer Space* sucked.

Last Jedi was far, far worse than a film that sucked. This was an abomination. This was an atrocity. This was a hollow desolation of the soul that deadens a little bit of the humanity of anyone who sees it.

Alas and alack and wailaway, but the thing showed up on Netflix, where I could see it free of charge, and it was a night when I was alone with no books in the room, and no computer to type on, and nothing else more productive to do with my time. I had no friend, no loved one, no loyal Japanese manservant, to stun me with the flat of a shovel and wrestle the remote control out of my fingers.

I said to myself, "I have been forewarned that this is bad; I am armed against disappointment. I am a man of stoical temper, stony-faced and ironclad of heart! Out of mere morbid curiosity, or to help me avoid pitfalls in penning my own space opera, this might be a way to beguile an idle two hours. Think of it as an autopsy!"

It was no autopsy. If you will imagine, as in some old black and white B-picture, a mad scientist with wild hair and wild eyes defying common sense and all laws of nature to haul a torpid vampire or slumbering zombie to the lab, thinking he could cut open and inspect the monster, only to have the horror rear up and rend him, you have seen my dire fate that dark night.

I thought I could take the blow of the stupidity hammer. I thought I was braced for it. And, yes, the stupidity hammer did come out of the screen and slam into my cortex, and lowered my IQ by a dozen points with each blow. I could feel myself getting stupider and stupider scene by scene, like that guy in the last half of *Flowers for Algernon*.

But the stupidity hammer was the rocket-powered spiked fifty-pound maul like something from *Battle Angel Alita*. And it did not just strike my head, but also my heart, and my soul.

It broke me. My nerve broke. Not only did I start fast-forwarding past whole scenes, but I switched the sound-track to a language I do not speak. I could still see the bad acting, but, thank heaven, I could no longer understand the asinine dialog.

So, keep this in mind: I did not see the whole film. I did not hear every line. This review therefore only reveals part, not all, of how unbearably bad it was. No matter what criticism or condemnation you hear from me in these pages, the reality is even worse.

Perhaps you have heard that Kathleen Kennedy, the head of the studio, say that she dislikes boyish space-adventure fiction and so decided not to film *Star Wars* as a space film. Rather, she meant *Last Jedi* to be a female-empowerment propaganda piece.

I have seen films that were also propaganda pieces: the 1949 *The Fountainhead* starring Gary Cooper, or the 1938 *Alexander Nevsky* directed by Sergei Eisenstein, with its brilliant score by Prokofiev. They actually did what propaganda films are supposed to do: hammer home a partisan point of view, using the story elements as tools to that end. The story telling is secondary to the partisan point, and sometimes is abandoned altogether.

Nonetheless, if done well, the end result can still be entertaining, as perhaps a well-constructed political homily might be. If done poorly, it is boring, hectoring, stiff and predictable, as absurd, uninspiring, and unpersuasive as a sermon by an atheist.

But there is a level of sheer, nose-stinging, eye-watering, foetid, mephitic, stinking, necromantic badness soaking through *Last Jedi* even more bad than merely mortal badness. This achieves a Zen Benightenment level of perfect, pellucid, pristine badness: a Platonic Ideal of a Bad Movie. It becomes immortal badness; ineffable badness; transcendental badness.

In this transcendental and ineffable void, one no longer can criticize the film by looking at why or how the filmmaker failed to achieve what he set out to do. You cannot tell what he set out to do. No theory of the filmmaker's intent makes sense. Nothing means anything.

But neither is the film boring in the way that watching meaningless acts of meaningless characters might be boring.

Last Jedi is not meaningless. It is mean.

The well-beloved old characters, and the stiffly cardboard-cutout new characters, are forced through antics and lines actively insulting to the viewer and humiliating to the cast and crew.

It was not because of total incompetence that this film descends to beneath the nadir. Total incompetence was there, to be sure. But malice played its part as well. This was a deconstruction of *Star Wars*, a character assassination against the franchise, and a shiv into the kidneys of the fans.

I would like to show that first, this was not a movie, and, second, this was not a female empowerment propaganda piece.

Let us walk, car by sad car, up and down the bloody and flaming trainwreck of this derailed circus train, inspecting the grotesque horror of the broken-necked giraffes, burst elephants, show dogs, and trick horses, and the mangled bodies of acrobats, sideshow freaks, and clowns.

To be a movie, it must have four elements:

First, it must tell a story. Stories boasting a plot have the purposes of characters clash, leading to conflict. Some dramatic matter must hang in the balance.

Second, characters are pretend people. For the pretense to seem real, the characters are supposed to act like people with recognizable personalities motivated by recognizable human emotions doing some sort of recognizable human action (preferably, a dramatic action) to reach some sort of recognizable human goal (preferably, a dramatic goal, where something is at stake).

The characters in a sci-fi yarn need not be human. They can be robots or aliens or whatever. But their personalities, emotions, actions, and goals must be something to which a human audience can relate.

Third, the plot is a set of pretend events. They happen because the writer says so. But they are supposed to create the illusion that they are happening according to their own internal cause and effect, arising out of causes that exist in the world, and leading to results that make some difference to the world. In a drama, the result should have emotional heft or weight that engages the audience. It should make some difference to them. It should have a point.

An adventure film has all these things plus action and thrills.

A space adventure has all these things but it takes place in a make-believe futuristic world where the tools and weapons and even the laws of nature work differently than what we currently know, but still stick closely to their own in-story logic. Even stories with space wizards working magic cannot have things happen for no reason.

Fourth, a sequel has all these things plus it keeps faith with what has come before. A sequel is supposed to fulfill the unspoken, understood promises of previous films. A *Star Wars* sequel has to fulfill the unspoken promises established by the prior films.

And if the franchise intends a sequel, there must be somewhere for the future plot to go. Driving the plot into a dead end where nothing is at stake and no drama is left, no mysteries unexplained, no potential for anything interesting to happen defeats this.

Lacking one of these four things, it is not a faithful Star Wars sequel film. Lacking each of these four things, it is not a film at all. It is an entertaining, bright, smelly mess that attracts attention. But so is a dumpster fire.

It should go without saying that a movie should also be technically proficient. The special effects should convince well enough to let the audience suspend willingly any disbelief. There should also to be a soundtrack of music suited to the material being presented. *Last Jedi* had the one but not the other.

Finally, in order to be a Female Empowerful propaganda effort, the story, or, rather, the allegory, must show the females having the power to accomplish typically male adventure deeds, such as fights, rescues, and escapes, as well or better than typical males.

However, this flick is so bad, each scene, practically each line, is such a studied insult and a wagging middle finger to the loyal fans delivered with such incompetent condescension by the film-maker, that a series of articles, or perhaps the rest of my natural life, might be required to do it justice.

1

BLIND CUTPURSE, DEAF SOUNDTRACK

By way of prologue, let me address and dismiss the elements of filmmaking of least interest to a science fiction writer like me: the mechanics of special effects, of which I know nothing, and the art of the sound track.

I am not a musician, but the barefoot teller of tales, and so it behooves me to dwell on those points where my opinion is expert opinion, plot, character, theme, world-building and so on. Where my opinion is superficial, it is better to speak briefly.

On the point of good special effects and visual spectacle only, *Last Jedi* held its own. Certain scenes were indeed spectacular, such as one where a ship rams a fleet at lightspeed, and obliterates a dozen war vessels in an act of dramatic kamikaze. Let us give credit where credit is due: that scene, and one or two others, did not betray the franchise legacy in terms of sheer visual splendor.

That one scene was sad to see, because it was promising. It looked good. (It made no sense, but it looked good). If this film had had a script, actors who could act, and had not been hellbent on insulting and heckling the fans, it might have stood a chance.

I am frankly surprised that of the many criticisms of this movie I've seen from many sources, only once chanced I upon another reviewer who panned the musical score. I thought the music was terrible, simply awful, in this film; but no one else seems to mind it.

I was bothered by the first note. The opening word crawl of *Star Wars* was punctuated by the brilliant trumpet flourishes of John William's famous overture. This word crawl has the same tune, but the sound is muted, the trumpets are mellow. It is lackluster.

Later in the film, when two characters enter the swanky, lavish casino of a Las Vegas planet, the music copies the sounds and theme from the cantina scene in *Star Wars*, as if the filmmaker cannot tell the difference between the tinkly, brassy, brash music one would play in a low-class dive, a wretched hive of scum and villainy, where pirates and roughnecks go to swill booze, and the swanky lounge music or torch songs played in posh nightclubs where the swells hang out.

Bubbly and beer are the same, right? So why not use the same music?

It was a lazy copy, an incompetent copy, where the filmmaker was trying to produce a certain effect, to set the mood of the scene via music, but picked the wrong music or did not know what mood to set.

Later still, in a scene where the Millennium Falcon is being chased through a maze of underground crystal plinths by screaming TIE fighter-craft, the exact same soundtrack, and I mean note-for-note the same, as is played during the Falcon's escape from the Death Star in the first one (you recall the scene: four fighters zooming in like WWI aces, and Luke and Han are manning the ack-ack guns. Luke cheers when it hits one, and Han warns him not to get cocky).

The problem is that the beats of the music in the original scene match the fighter-pilot turns, gun blasts, and camera changes as adroitly as Ginger Rogers following Fred Astaire's footwork backward in heels.

But in this one, the music is not matched to anything, so the sudden crescendos or trumpet flourishes happen when nothing is happening, and crashes and explosions happen when the music is monotonic or falling. It sounds off. It is a copy copied as if by an idiot, who cannot tell what he is copying or why.

We shall see below how the filmmaker here is a blind cutpurse, who steals the purse, the surface features alone, but leaves the gold coins at the heart of the purse that give it heft and value, and which alone make the purse worth stealing.

2

NOT A WORD CRAWL

L et us begin at the beginning. A film must have a story. This did not. It had a fight scene, a chase scene, and a fight scene. Other stuff happened, none of which made any difference or made any sense.

For purposes of comparison, *Star Wars* (the film you young whippersnappers call *A New Hope*) has a story. It is tightly plotted, simple and clear, with clear motives and goals, a dramatic clash of plot and counterplot, cunning twists, culminating in an explosive and satisfying climax.

The story starts from the first note of trumpets. Here is the opening word crawl to *Star Wars*:

It is a period of civil war.
Rebel spaceships, striking
from a hidden base, have won
their first victory against
the evil Galactic Empire.
During the battle, Rebel
spies managed to steal secret
plans to the Empire's
ultimate weapon, the DEATH

*STAR, an armored space
station with enough power to
destroy an entire planet.
Pursued by the Empire's
sinister agents, Princess
Leia races home aboard her
starship, custodian of the
stolen plans that can save
her people and restore
freedom to the galaxy.....*

It is not easy to write a good word crawl. Believe you me, it takes rare skill and pulp genius to reach this level of simplicity, clarity, and punch. The plot hook is deeply set by the time the last word floats upward on the screen. By then, the audience is engaged.

It is four sentences. It establishes four things: (1) Plot: civil war between rebels and the evil empire. (2) McGuffin: the secret plans to the ultimate weapon. (3) Character: Space princess, pursued by sinister agents. (4) Motive: She wants to save her people and restore freedom to the galaxy.

For those of you unfamiliar with the term, a 'McGuffin' was Alfred Hitchcock's slang for the widget driving the plot: the purloined letter, diamond necklace, holy grail, or secret plans the cops or crooks or knights or spies chasing each other care about, even if the audience does not. The Maltese Falcon is a McGuffin, as is the One Ring, the Ark of the Covenant, or the Queen's diamond studs she unwisely gave to the Duke of Buckingham.

The brevity and panache of these opening lines in *Star Wars* allow us to move right into the desperate fight scene where the monstrously huge interstellar warship, engines throbbing, is swallowing up the wounded ship of the Princess, and her soldiers, loyal unto death to her, sweating with fear, take up hopeless firing positions before the burning airlock doors that the sinister agents of the Empire are about to force open...

Thanks to the word crawl, we know what is at stake, what the opposing sides want so desperately, and why.

Here is the opening of *Last Jedi*.

The FIRST ORDER reigns.
Having decimated the peaceful
Republic, Supreme Leader Snoke
now deploys his merciless
legions to seize military
control of the galaxy.
Only General Leia Organa's
band of RESISTANCE fighters
stand against the rising
tyranny, certain that Jedi
Master Luke Skywalker will
return and restore a spark of
hope to the fight.
But the Resistance has been
exposed. As the First Order
speeds toward the rebel base,
the brave heroes mount a
desperate escape....

From the first line of the first frame in the first minute of the film, its badness is displayed. Instead of an Evil Empire, we have something called the First Order, perhaps one of the least menacing names ever.

The First Order, confusingly enough, are not the established power running the galaxy, but rebels overthrowing the Republic in order to restore Imperial government, which would make it the Second Order, if it were anything.

Instead of the Princess, a title that conjures romance and

mystery, Leia is now merely a General. A confusing demo-
tion. (A question for the fathers of four-year-old girls out
there: how many of your daughters daydream about being
generals rather than princesses?) So, the Princess is not a
princess.

The Republic, even more confusingly, is not the republic, and not even anything cool-sounding like the Rebellion,
but something called the Resistance, one of the least
inspiring names ever. Rebellion topples kings and erects
new forms of government. Resistance is a sullen slow-down:
mere foot-dragging. It makes them sound like Protest
Marchers rather than like Minutemen and Founding
Fathers.

The Resistance has been "exposed" which makes even
less sense—since this is allegedly the legitimate democrati-
cally-elected government of the galaxy.

But the word crawl both says that the Republic has been
decimated—note past tense—and that Supreme Leader
Snoopy is in the act of unleashing his merciless legions to
seize military control—note present tense. Which is it? It
Supreme Leader Snoopy taking over, or has he taken over?

And the brave heroes are bravely mounting, not a
counter-attack, or a desperate last stand, but instead—wait
for it—a desperate escape.

But if the Republic is the legitimate government of the
Galaxy, why are they crouched on a rebel base rather than
occupying the Pentagon, or NORAD, or whatever the name
might be of the main space-marine super-fortress of the
capital planet?

This is a pointless confusion. It all could be cleared up in
a single sentence, and by calling things by their right names.
It could fill in what happened after the end of *Return of the
Jedi* and before the opening of *Force Awakens*. Instead, the

filmmaker evidently wanted the heroes to be the underdogs in rebellion against space tyrants once again, because making up something new might require a brain. So, the victory crowning the beloved first trilogy is simply whisked away without explanation.

(Frodo goes back to the Shire, and then, on Tuesday, he falls out of bed, and finds that Sauron has sprung back to life and taken over Gondor, Mirkwood, Eriador, and erected his new Dark Tower in Bree, where he forges STARKILLER RING, a version of the One Ring twice the size of the first.)

The words of this word crawl have an atmosphere of lazy incompetence, as if someone is trying to copy an original he does not understand, so he copies inconsequential elements or surface features. Here again, he is the blind cutpurse who pilfers the bag but leaves the gold coins behind.

This is something we will see throughout: nearly every element in this film is a lazy copy that misses the point of the original.

The point of an opening word crawl is to sum up the situation clearly and quickly enough that you can start the plot *in media res*, that is, in mid-action, without lengthy explanations of who is chasing whom and why.

This word crawl simply does not do that. This word crawl establishes nothing: there is no McGuffin. There is nothing driving the plot, nothing to kick-start the action.

It is vague rather than clear. It is bland.

Note the difference between saying "he is seizing military control of the galaxy" versus something like, "His troops conquered the galactic capital planet Coruscant. The bold loyalists must flee the ruins of Coruscant with the remnant of their fleet, or be destroyed". Or the difference between saying, "Jedi Master Luke Skywalker will return and restore a spark of hope to the fight" versus something like, "Unless Jedi Master Luke Skywalker is found in time, all hope is lost. Only he can battle evil space wizard Kylo Ren!"

The last paragraph tells us that the bad guys' fleet is closing in on the Rebel Base, and the rebels are running away. But this is established in the next shot, and there is nothing else that needed to be said, so the word crawl is wasted.

What are those other paragraphs there for?

The General is waiting for the Jedi Master to "restore a spark of hope." Unlike when (in the original) she was being chased by sinister agents while carrying secret plans to an ultimate weapon, her waiting around for someone else to cheer up the troops does not have any obvious military value. Who cares?

Nor is any reason given why the bad guys would act to stop the waiting for the Jedi Master from happening, or stop the Jedi Master. In fact, the bad guys do not act to stop it from happening. This is not a point of conflict in the plot. In fact, he is not coming.

A conflict is when a character acts to get something he wants, or to avoid something he fears, and his antagonist acts in opposition. Where there is no opposition, there is no conflict. No conflict, no drama. So why mention it?

And what does "restoring a spark of hope" mean? It sounds like it means the rebellion has bad morale. That does not make them sound like heroes.

And if they find this one guy, what? Everyone's face lights up? They take heart?

Space Opera plots are supposed to center around clear, simple, and serious things, such as secret plans for the ultimate weapon, kidnapped princesses, revenge, corruption, despair, hope, redemption. Waiting for hope is not serious enough to be a space opera plot.

Let me show you what I mean:

Only General Leia Organa's
band of RESISTANCE fighters
stand against the rising
tyranny, certain that funnyman Bob Hope
and the beautiful blonde Marilyn Monroe
will put on a USO show for the troops,
lift their lagging spirits,
and restore a spark of
hope to the fight.

I note that this word crawl contains some misleading statements.

General Leia Organa's band of RESISTANCE fighters, in fact, do not take any stand against the rising tyranny, nor is any tyranny on stage. There is no scene of Dark Helmet choking a member of the Ambassador's staff without due process of law, and no scene of Luke's family being gunned down without a warrant.

Indeed, the only scene I can bring to mind of unlawful and terrorist acts is when a lunatic dwarf woman in order to avoid paying a traffic ticket unleashes a stampede of space-racehorses into a casino to trample innocent patrons, croupiers, and cocktail waitresses and do untold property damage. Unfortunately, she was one of the aforementioned Resistance fighters. More on this later.

The First Order, in fact, did not seize military control of the galaxy: in the prior movie, five planets within naked eyesight range of each other were blown up, evidently five satellites of the same gas giant or something. Nothing implied that those five planets contained the whole leadership of the Republic, leaving the countless worlds of the galaxy suddenly leaderless. Indeed, that is the whole resilience of a republican form of government. The leader is not the king. If you shoot the president, the vice president or leader of the Senate takes over, or the people just elect new leaders.

Nor could the FIRST ORDER seize military control of jack. They are not the Empire, and do not have hundreds of robot-manned factory worlds to crank out endless ships, or endless clone armies. As best I can tell, they are a small group of malcontents who do not realize the civil war ended thirty years ago. When the Starkiller base is blown up, countless troops and materiel are obliterated. This includes Captain Phasmid, or whatever her name is, in her chrome armor. Last we saw, she was thrown in a trash compacter and then the world the trash compactor happens to be on is obliterated in a cosmic explosion. (She shows up later with no dents in her armor.)

However, the filmmaker throughout treats the First Order as if it were the Empire, and has all of its resources and terrifying strength. The filmmaker forgets that the Republic is the legitimate government, and calls them the Resistance, but then says they occupy rebel bases, and has them called rebels throughout. Again, this is an unnecessary confusion and a sign of lazy writing. For the purpose of clarity and to mock the lazy writing, in this column, I will call the doofus bad guys the Empire, and call the doofus good guys the Rebels. Because, why not?

So much for the first one minute of screen time. As the word crawl ends, the film goes downhill rapidly from there.

3

NOT AN OPENING SCENE

Now, in theory, the plot here should have involved the same two plotlines we saw and loved in *Empire Strikes Back*, which is the film that the filmmaker is lazily copying and malignly mocking.

There, in *Empire Strikes Back*, the rebels (including Space Princess and Lovable Rogue, Space Bigfoot, and comedy relief robots) are driven from their hidden base, and are fleeing a Starfleet dreadnought, who is pursuing them through raging asteroid fields and across the galaxy.

Meanwhile, Space Farmboy finds the Jedi Master Muppet, receives training, but rushes unwisely to confront the evil Lord Dark Helmet before his training is complete: disaster follows, and Luke is maimed, but escapes with his life.

There are plot twists when Lovable Rogue meets his old friend Unlikely Ally in Floaty City, there is treason and counter-treason; there is a growing romance between Space Princess and Lovable Rogue. Starfleet is not merely chasing the rebels to kill them, but because the sinister Emperor plans to capture Space Farmboy, now a young Jedi, and turn him to the Dark Side.

There are four character arcs: Farmboy goes from being a novice to a knight; Rogue goes from being a loner to a lover; Space Princess goes from being too cold to warm; Unlikely Ally goes from being a false friend to a true one.

The two threads combine in a climax when Luke defiantly flies to Floaty City to save his friends, but falls into a trap, and learns the terrible secret of his parentage. Lovable Rogue is abducted by sinister Bounty Hunter, and the tense plot is *To be Continued* on some warm summer matinee far, far away...

Despite the deceptively cartoonish simplicity of the theme, the plot here is fast-paced, clear, clever, engaging, and at times reaches the dignity of a Greek Tragedy. Brilliant writing.

Here, in *The Last Jedi*, the rebels (including Hotshot Pilot, Tweedledim the Token Stormtrooper, Tweedledank the zoink-powered Wrench Monkey, space hag General Ruin, and space crone Girl-General Gender Studies van Grievance of the Purple Hair) are driven from their hidden base by a clowncar of Space Nazis led by a Sith Wanker and a Bad Muppet named Snoopy. Call this non-plot C.

Meanwhile, Mary Sue the Perfect Girl finds Jedi Master Mopey Sulkwalker, who is moping. She wants him to help and he refuses. Because mopey. She rushes off to confront the whiny and unthreatening pasty-faced Sith wanker, Emo Vader, or whatever his name was. Mopey Sulkwalker is happy to see her go. Call this non-plot B.

Mary Sue thinks she can turn Emo Vader to the Sunny Side, while he thinks he can turn her to the Dim Side. Or maybe he thinks he can get her to change her expression. SPOILERS! She doesn't and he can't.

Tweedledim and Wrench Monkey go for no particular reason to a casino, endanger innocent bystanders, fail to free a slave-boy who aids them, and run away from the traffic cops. Call this non-plot A. Maybe this was meant to be a side-quest, but it took up most of the running time and sucked all the oxygen out of the room.

There are events that suddenly happen for no reason, which I guess were meant to count as plot twists. A murder, a mutiny, a suicide, a stampede, a betrayal, but who cares? If there is supposed to be a growing romance between Emo Vader and Mary Sue, or between Tweedledim and Tweedledank, I missed it.

Nothing was surprising because nothing was actually happening, and nothing actually made sense.

The three threads combine into a stupid snarl of nonsense at the end when Tweedledim beats up his evil drill sergeant Phasmid, then tries to sacrifice himself but doesn't. Meanwhile, Emo Vader fights Mopey Sulkwalker except he doesn't, and Mary Sue opens a blocked cave exit that no one else could have opened except they could have, and they all run away. More. Just as they had been doing throughout. Back to square one. Call this the non-Climax.

Do you notice what is missing from this plot? A plot. Events, of a sort, have happened, but nothing is resolved, nothing is accomplished, and nothing means anything. There are no character arcs.

More to the point, and it is a damning point, every source of plot tension, every dramatic question engaging the audience and driving the plot forward has been derailed and deflated in what can only be called an ongoing act of insolent auctorial malfeasance.

Everything, and I mean *everything*, of any interest inherited from the prior films is systematically robbed of any drama or point, so that there is no possibility of any sequel to this dog. More on this later.

In *Empire Strikes Back*, the assault on the rebel base on the Ice Planet in the first reel is one of the best set-pieces in the trilogy of films, where the walking tanks of the Empire, the AT-ATs, come lumbering over the snow, unstoppable juggernauts.

In this film...?

The assault on the rebel base begins with Hotshot Pilot going alone in a one-man fighter to a point just off the prow of the main enemy battleship, and putting in a prank radio call to the evil fleet admiral. The evil fleet admiral does something neither Grand Moff Tarkin, nor Darth Vader, nor any other officer of the evil Galactic Empire ever has been seen doing: he rants and boasts like a scenery-chewing supervillain. He starts monologuing.

Hotshot Pilot then pretends to have a bad connection, and asks again to speak to the fleet admiral to whom he is speaking. He calls him Admiral Hugs instead of his name, which is Hux. The evil fleet admiral checks his microphone.

This deflates whatever impressive menace the threats of the villain may have had, and makes the admiral look like a feckless boob. They repeat this routine two or three times, *ad nauseam*. Hotshot makes an unfunny 'Yo Mama' joke.

I assume writer/director Rian Johnson, the filmmaker (or, rather, the film-perpetrator) wanted this to come across as a bit of bold and buoyant swashbuckler's defiance, something as when the Errol Flynn version of Robin Hood is seen walking right into the Sheriff of Nottingham's castle during a feast, with the carcass of an illegally poached king's deer slung gaily over his shoulders, swinging the horned head and hoofs so as to knock aside the guards sent to stop him, and slyly mocking his host by asking whether the guards were beggars so hungry they tried to steal his meat.

This was not sly, nor gay, nor defiant, nor bold, nor anything. It was lame, tin-earned, unfunny, and stupid. It was like what a man with no sense of humor might try to do when told to write a funny quip.

So, the mood is set immediately: The Empire is no threat, and the Hotshot Pilot is in no danger. Nothing matters. No humor, no thrills.

We are now two, perhaps three, minutes into the film. An infinity of minutes equally as free of entertainment value await.

Shooting starts. Explosions. For some reason, a titanic space-battleship the size of an aircraft carrier cannot blow up or shoot down a dinky one-man space-fighter the size of a jetplane. Hotshot easily destroys all their hull-mounted deck guns, but, for some dumb reason never explained, not the honking big cannon used to blast the whole rebel base to smithereens in one shot.

Meanwhile, on the planet surface (you guessed it) the rebel base is blasted to smithereens in one shot. So, nothing the fighters did in outer space overhead matters. But the explosion catches no one, since everyone already in the refugee flotilla flying away, so nothing the attacking force does matters either.

This sets the pattern of everything to follow: all fights are one-punch affairs, where defeat is instant or victory is instantaneous, as if the film-perpetrator were bored with the idea of portraying the effort and sacrifice, tactics, courage, stubbornness, and cunning needed to fight a fight.

I have heard other reviewers compliment these fight scenes. I have never seen any more boring. Each was obvious at the outset who would handily defeat whom.

None had the least trace of any thought put into it. No victory required effort or sacrifice.

Leia, at one time one of my favorite characters of all time, but now an absurd Feminist Empowerful sideshow clown, appears on screen. She is a woman who managed to give birth to pasty-faced Dad-killing Emo Vader, then to have her marriage shipwreck into divorce, and who managed to orchestrate the second downfall of the Republic in her lifetime, except now it is on her watch and under her leadership. She managed to make all the struggles and sacrifice of her life, and the lives of her friends and fellows, utterly meaningless. She has lost everything, and what little she had left in this flick, she loses. Everything is left in general ruin.

She is also the worst leader of all time, including Rufus T. Firefly. I cannot abide to call her by the beloved name of my once-favorite character, so let us refer to her as General Ruin. The word also sums up her make-up, costume, lines, and the fond memories of her long career.

(Let us pause to pity the poor actress, may she rest in peace, who could have done a perfectly fine job if the make-up lady and costume department had not been against her, or the writers given her some real lines to say. Pity for the character, however, not a drop. Carrie Fisher I like. General Ruin I hate.)

General Ruin calls Hotshot Pilot on the radio and tells him to break off the attack. Why? To save on men and supplies. (But then why order the attack in the first place?) But he has to knock out the very last deck gun, in order to allow the bombers to get close. (Was that the plan from the beginning? If not, why have the bombers standing by?)

The warship he is attacking is a dreadnought, which he describes as a 'fleet-killer'. If he is right, the Rebels have no choice but to attack it, no matter what the cost, since the alternative is certain death for the whole escape flotilla. But then his general is an idiot for telling him to break off; and if not right, he is the idiot. In either case, they cannot both be heroes in a space opera. Getting loyal servicemen killed pointlessly, just as much as running from a necessary fight, is a gross defect in leadership appropriate only to a nihilistic anti-war statement film.

So, Hotshot, in an act of gross insubordination, ignores the order! Hotshot hotly flips his radio switch off! And she for no reason fails to radio her orders to the other ships! Maybe his switch was extra-hotshot or something, and it shut down her broadcaster, not his receiver! Which makes no sense!

But suddenly his weapons are offline! Sparks are leaking from an electrical panel in the back!

Annoying robot Billiard Ball, in an unfunny comedy relief bit, sticks his robot finger into the electrical panel like the Little Dutch Boy trying to plug a hole in the dike, so that whenever he stops the sparks from leaking in one spot, another stream of sparks leaks out in another. Annoying robot Billiard Ball smacks its head into the panel and the delicate electrical circuits are suddenly back in working order! (I felt my first five IQ points of the many I was fated to lose this evening gush out of my ears under the blow of the rocket-powered stupidity hammer that came out of the screen at that moment and pounded me between the eyes.) Hotshot hotly shoots the final deck gun.

Then bombers fly up. Except there is no "up" in the zero-gravity conditions of outer space. In space, bombs, if let free, would simply follow the inertial momentum of the ship carrying them, until such time as the ship accelerated, turned, or decelerated, which would therefore not be a bomber in any sense of the word.

The bomber pilots arm all the bombs while still in the bomb bays, not (as in real life) only once they are clear. Clearly, bomber pilots in this universe suffer from a death wish. A wish immediately granted! Butterfingered bomber pilots immediately ram into each other, blowing two of the ships up in a vast fireball of special effects, and then debris from a damaged fighter smashes into the third one, so it goes up like a firecracker.

In an instant, without any effort on the part of the Empire, there is only one bomber left. Then that ship's butterfingered bomber pilot is killed, so that the bombardier, an attractive oriental woman, after she opens the bomb bay doors (which open into the hard vacuum of outer space) has to climb up the absurdly tall ladder from the bomb doors to the pilot's seat, and find the TV remote control which has the big red button to drop the bombs.

Why she does not flip off the artificial gravity and sail up to the cabin is unclear.

For some reason, there is no manual switch at the bombardier's station to drop the bombs, despite that dropping bombs is what a bombardier does, so you would think that if anyone had the switch, she would.

She climbs heroically, with much desperate brave heroic climbing, then falls heroically because she is a butterfingers, and is lying on her broken back, so she has to kick the ladder heroically with her tiny, slender, shapely oriental legs, and the hundred-foot-tall ladder shakes free from its moorings, and this drops the TV remote past her hand and out the space window into outer space (which continues to be hard vacuum), but then, HEADFAKE! the remote for no reason is still within reach and so she catches it anyway! Now she can push the button, but then she and her ship blow up for no reason, so she dies, but the bombs fall (in zero-gravity) down (in zero-gravity) and strike the battleship, blowing it to bits.

Except this victory is, one scene later, said to be pointless. A Pyrrhic victory.

The big ship is destroyed in one shot by the one remaining bomber, but the rebel base is destroyed one moment earlier in one barrage by the big cannon, so all that fight scene was basically pointless. So, the only good-looking actress in this whole film had her character die for nothing!

This is a recurring theme. Everything is for nothing.

I admit I was confused by the sight of the good-looking oriental actress, since other reviewers told me the oriental diversity hire in this film was an ugly, slab-faced, dank, and dumpy dwarf with bad hair.

Long after, I was informed that all the characters we saw dying in the opening five minutes of the film, people given few lines to say, or none, spear-carriers and extras with no background, and no reason for anyone in the audience to give a hoot, were all taken from Disney's other material they are using to replace the Expanded Universe.

These are apparently books and comics the film perpetrator meant you, the audience, to read first, as homework, in order to get the full emotional impact of the death scenes of perfect strangers.

I will pass without comment over the sheer ineptitude, the sheer laziness, the Mary Sue style writing which relies on the audience being familiar with other stories and plot points established in other material not provided with the ticket price. Like a politician or a rock star getting a round of applause merely by asking the audience to clap for their own hometown, the lazy writer relies on someone else's work to do the work of setting up emotional depth and plot-logic that the film-perp here merely exploits lazily.

We next see General Ruin as she is bitch-slapping Hotshot Pilot, telling him that there are problems one cannot solve by jumping in fighter-craft and blowing something up.

True, blowing things up does not solve the Ellsberg paradox of game-theory nor the three-body problem in physics.

It does, of course, solve exactly type of military problems (like the problem of evil space battleships of an evil space empire coming to kill you) which the military is meant to solve, and which, as best I can tell, Hotshot Pilot did solve, when he blew to heck the giant ship coming to kill them all.

He is demoted from Commodore to Dogcatcher on the spot. No court martial, no military courtesy, no explanation. Normally a court martial is dramatic, because the hero is basically losing his career, but here, the whole thing is basically pointless, since his duties and privileges, as best I can tell, are unchanged.

Which means the scene where he is slapped and demoted for doing his duty is pointless, merely idiotic leadership on the part of an hysterical and overwrought woman. But her character was never shown to suffer from such gross lapses of judgement before.

Perhaps in a nihilistic antiwar-statement flick, this would be appropriate. It is not the way a heroine in a Buck Rogers serial acts. Wilma Deering would be ashamed.

But if, on the other hand, he overestimated the striking power of the dreadnought, then he got soldiers and sailors under his command killed pointlessly, in that case his decision was criminally negligent. But his character was never shown to suffer from such gross dereliction of duty before.

So, as of the end of the first scene, nothing makes sense, and nothing has a point.

We will see this as a repeating pattern.

4

NON-PLOT A: TWEEDLEDIM AND TWEEDLEDANK

Next we see Token Stormtrooper, hereafter to be called Tweedledim, waking up in a medical bed with a comical look of surprise on his face.

My memory says that he was seriously, nigh-fatally, injured in a serious, nigh-fatal, duel with a Sith in the previous episode. A broken spine or something. But, suddenly, and for no reason, no pain, no recovery, no recuperation is shown. Maybe the guy was just malingering.

He immediately bumps his head. Then he pulls tubes out of himself, so that oozy white fluid sloshes over him, so that when he gets up, he slips on the ooze, and takes a pratfall. There are no nurses, doctors, or medical robots anywhere in sight.

I assume this scene was meant to be slapstick comedy, to show that even in outer space, black men are clumsy, craven, and silly rather than cool, manly, and competent like Mace Windu or Lando Calrissian.

Stepin Fetchit was asked to play this part and do this scene, but he thought it was demeaning to the dignity of the Negro race. But Stepin Fetchit was actually good at his craft, and he could have done the slapstick comedy better than Tweedledim.

However, the problem I had watching this, and the reason my brain kept silently screaming at the shock of the nine-pound sledge hammer of stupidity that would reach out of the screen and slam me between the eyes, was that my reeling brain could shoot blood and gray matter out of my ears, but it could not figure out what the film-perpetrator meant the scene to accomplish.

Why turn the one could-have-been-interesting character, a stormtrooper who defects from the Empire, into a silly-willy fumble-dummy, whose only purpose is to slip on the soap and take a pratfall? Was it meant to show that he is a clown and not a hero? Was it meant to show that his injuries were not serious, the film was not serious, and that nothing mattered?

Now, throughout the prior film all Tweedledim tried to do was cower, flee, and run away. When he volunteered to return to Starkiller Base at risk to life and limb, I thought that character arc was complete. But no: someone hit the reset button. He is back to his old self, unchanged at the beginning of this film.

He sneaks down to the escape pods with his rucksack, about to abandon ship (apparently intending to float into the waiting guns of the Imperial Deathfleet, which is in hot pursuit immediately behind), when suddenly an ugly, slab-faced, dumpy, dwarf with bad hair flourishing a cattleprod stumps out from where she is cleaning toilets or something.

I could not tell what her rank or duty was. Let's assume she is ground crew: a Wrench Monkey. She says her job is to wrestle and stun any of the rebel soldierboys, all gorillas built like linebackers, to prevent them from using the escape pods to flee, because, of course, heroes and good guys not only flee like cowards, but heroic good guy armies whip them back into the fight like orcs. No volunteer army, this!

And who else would you have as the bouncer or the Shore Patrol guarding the escape pods? Big, beefy marines? A war-bot with 9mm infinite repeater blasterguns? Or the midget Wrench Monkey with a cattleprod to zoink people?

This, not the attractive girl, was the diversity hire the other reviewers complained about. Their complaints were understated. This character was a towering ninny and a nincompoop, dunderfaced and dampwitted, and I was rooting for stormtroopers to shoot her in her big, whiny mouth.

(Let us pause to pity the poor actress, who could have been perfectly serviceable if dressed nicely and given decent lines to say or something interesting to do. But pity for the character, not a drop.)

She is first seen crying uncontrollably, like all good soldiers. It turns out this girl is that hot bombardier girl's sister, who died for nothing thanks to the incompetence of General Ruin, butterfingered bomber pilots, and Hotshot. So, I suppose this was maybe meant to make the audience feel sorry for her. Or maybe not.

Because any sorrow is immediately countermanded by her behavior in the scene where she is introduced: she immediately starts gushing over Tweedledim, the Token Stormtrooper, calling him a great hero of the rebellion for his role in the last movie, when he was standing around while Starkiller Base blew up.

He puts aside his natural embarrassment, and pretends to be a hero, and pretends to be (ahem) inspecting the escape pod. With his rucksack. He tells her to go her way. She slowly catches on, because she is a dimwit, and, because he is clumsy and incompetent, she manages to zoink him with her cattleprod, and we are treated to the sight of his body being flung across the cabin, and get a porthole-eye closeup view of his buttocks slamming into the glass.

Once again, through the fog of blood droplets and brain matter from my exploding cranium, as I am battered yet again through the skull by the stupidity hammer, I also cannot figure out what the film-perpetrator meant to accomplish from this scene.

Was it supposed to be funny? It was not. Humor would have been exactly the wrong note to play when soldier finds another trying to turn deserter, especially one she thinks is a great and brave hero. That goes double for a soldier who just lost a sibling to the cause.

Was it supposed to be cynical? It was not. Tweedledank the Zoink Dwarf is discovering her idol has feet of clay, and it should have been a moment of grim shock to her, not a moment of slapstick zany.

Was it supposed to be sad? It was not. We meet a woman whose sister just gave the last full measure of self-sacrifice for their sacred cause of freedom, so a little bit of sobriety may have been called for. If we are meant to take that self-sacrifice seriously. Are we? Because having the comedy relief fall-on-buttocks pratfall erases any seriousness needed for a sad scene.

Was it supposed to show the Tweedledim, Token Stormtrooper, is a scatterbrained nincompoop? All Dim had to do was say he was on a secret mission for the Space Princess, and Dank would no doubt have let him pass.

Was it supposed to show Tweedledank, Zoink Dwarf, is worse than a nincompoop? It does accomplish that, because it also shows that she has a sadistic streak, because we see her dragging Tweedledim away on a gurney, while he whines and moans that he is paralyzed. Apparently he took spinal damage right where the Sith knight struck him in the last movie with a plasma-hot lightsaber, and so is paralyzed for life, but this is played for laughs.

Imagine how much more stature, and, yes, character development, would have been displayed in this dumb scene if Dank had realized that Dim was turning deserter, and, because of her unrequited hero-worship of his figure, she had straightened her spine and said, "Take me with you!"—and if he, touched by this show of faith from a woman who barely knows him, had suddenly looked grim, taken back his rucksack, and said, "I am not going anywhere." And he returned to his post.

Except, actually, he does not have a post. Unless I missed a scene in the last movie where he took the Rebel's Oath or enlisted or swore fealty to the Princess, he is not actually a serviceman in the Republican army. And he can be beaten up by a Wrench Monkey with a zoink wand. So, this scene shows he is weak, cowardly, and stupid, all at once.

Now, persons watching the film more closely than I might tell you that Tweedledim actually had a profound and selfless motivation. Because of his great affection for Mary Sue (an affection nowhere in evidence in the prior film, or invisible to me) he wants to take the tracking device Mary Sue gave General Ruin, steal it, and spirit it away to some other location, so that Mary Sue, once she returns with Master Jedi Luke Skywalker in tow, the only hope anyone has for victory, will wander the starways aimlessly, unable to find the rebels again. Um. Because Dim thinks Mary Sue will be in danger if she rejoins the rebels.

Maybe this plot point was in the film or maybe not. I cannot honestly say, and I hated this film so much that even though, with the touch of a button, I could call it up on my Netflix app right this second to check, I am unwilling to expose my tender brain to the ravages of the stupidity hammer again.

Because if that were Dim's motivation, it is a stupid and cowardly motivation, unworthy of mention in a space opera manned by heroes, and it has no effect whatsoever on the plot.

The tracking device does not turn out to be an Imperial tracker allowing Starfleet to track them through hyperspace, nor is Mary Sue ever shown needing anything to find the rebels in flight: she just shows up.

And since, at the end of the film, Dim and the tracker and Mary Sue and the rebels are all in one spot anyway, nothing comes of Dim's alleged attempt to separate the two.

Nor does he throw the tracking device out the space window into space, to have it fall down, the direction the bombs from the bombers fell, nor does his step on it with his space boot and crush it, nor does he take a space screwdriver, unscrew the nano-neutronium annunular confinement cover plate and remove the hyper dilithium space battery. Nor does he hand it to a slaveboy groom on the Swank Casino planet he visits later.

He does nothing with it. The writer forgot about it. Nothing makes sense. Nothing matters.

I suppose it is nice to look after your friend, but to ruin her sacred mission to recruit the last Jedi in the galaxy in order to save her life shows the same freakish reversal of disordered priorities which, ironically, we are going to see at the very end of this film, except with him in the position of the person being saved from his own duty by a stalker.

In any case, if that were his motivation, he is still shown to be a feckless dope in the scene where he carried out his plan, and is carried out on a gurney with a bent spine.

Next, we see Hotshot Pilot, now demoted to Dogcatcher,

for no reason (nothing in the film happens for a reason) wander absentmindedly into to the pod bay where the Dank is hauling the whining, weeping Dim around on a gurney. Ask your friends in the Navy how often fighter pilot captains wander into the bilge decks without being on duty, and why no one in the Republic military salutes, and why no one reports deserters to any authority, and likewise when a soldier-girl assaults a fellow soldier with a cattleprod and zoinks him, there is no inquiry, no one is put on report, and nothing comes of it.

For no reason (nothing in the film happens for a reason), Hotshot discusses the fact that the Empire has discovered a new technology that allows them to track fleeing starships through hyperspace, something that was impossible in the previous films.

The Token Stormtrooper Tweedledim, and the Zoink-Happy Wrench Monkey Tweedledank, suddenly and for no reason know so much about theoretical cutting-edge subspace tracking positronic systems that they can deduce, from no information whatsoever, the specifications and limitations of the new invention.

These specifications and limitations are, as everything else in this film, stupid: Apparently, this new tracking system can only be run from a single machine on a single starship. They have to sneak aboard the lead starship of the pursuing fleet, find the McGuffin, and discombobulate it.

The discombobulation will last six minutes and only six: in that amount of time, while the desperate clock is ticking, will be the last and only hope of the Rebel flotilla to make its escape!

Remember that time limit. Six minutes! Remember it with all your braincells! Because nothing whatsoever will come of it, and it means nothing.

So now, the McGuffin, which should have been mentioned in the opening word-crawl, not only comes on stage, but no spies, no, not even a single Bothan, needed to die to get its operational specs. The comedy relief crew of Tweedles can figure it all out on the fly.

Seriously, did anyone, ANYONE, read this dog's breakfast of a script? You put the McGuffin in the opening word crawl, and make that the plot hook:

It is a dark time for the Rebellion.
Although the Starkiller Base has been destroyed,
Imperial troops hound the dwindling Rebel forces.
A new long-range spy-ray system,
known as the OMNITRON,
Can track ships through hyperspace
and expose the location of hidden rebel bases.
Only one MASTER CODEBREAKER
might know the secret
to defeat the all-seeing Omnitron.
But can he be found in time...?
Or whatever.

So now we have Hotshot Pilot, listening to the technobabble pour out of two people who could not possibly know this info, holo-telephone the barkeeper from the last movie, who was the yellow-skinned bug-eyed Yoda-substitute wise old lady.

Why telephone her, of all people, instead of the chief of Naval Intelligence, or his commanding officer, or his mom, or even Jar Jar Binks? No reason.

The bartender is in the middle of a shooting war. We see her holo-telephone image doing backflips while blaster bolts zap and zoink at her from each direction. She is in no danger whatsoever. We do not see her attackers, but they are apparently spastic yet clumsy lobotomy-victims all blind in one eye.

Once again, I could not puzzle out what the film-perpetrator had in mind. Why have the heroes watch the bartender in a running firefight through the phone?

If it was to stop the bartender from helping them because she was too busy, then the gunmen have to be a threat. Otherwise, she can just skip and dance lightly away whenever she wishes. (But why not simply have her say she herself does not have the code-breaking skills needed to help them, but she knows of someone else who does?)

But if the gunmen are indeed a threat, the heroes, if they are heroes, need to express some concern for her well-being, and speak about getting a squad of marines there to help her. Instead they stand around with their mouths open, looking bewildered and incompetent.

So apparently this scene is meant for laughs, except it is not funny. Her coolness under pressure does not mean anything if she is not under pressure.

Nothing ever comes of the bartender's fight-scene. It is merely background noise.

She tells them that to the discombobulate the McGuffin, they need a Master Codebreaker, of which there is only one in the whole galaxy: he patronizes a swank casino on Swank Casino Planet, and he can be identified because he wears a puce carnation in his lapel. The bartender cannot give his name, race, height, weight, or any other distinguishing features: but she does happen to have a picture of the puce carnation she can transmit.

No explanation is given as to how bartender knows the codebreaker, and knows his lapel pin, but does not know his name, race, height, weight, or any other distinguishing features.

The shtick with the carnation is a lazy writer's trick to allow for an additional level of tension, or humor value, springing from mistaken identities. But in this case, nothing comes of this.

The scene made no sense and accomplished nothing. The bartender was not needed. The ex-Stormtrooper Dim could have said, "I am familiar with that McGuffin project: there was one codebreaker who escaped from us, who knows the secret. He can be found on planet Swank, etc." or, more to the point, why not have the Wrench Monkey Dank say, "I have a master's degree in ansible electro-photonics. I can discombobulate it."

Then more stupid happens. The Hotshot Dogcatcher, who is the Commanding Officer of no one in the scene, now orders Tweedledim and Tweedledank to go to planet Swank and find the Codebreaker, come back, disguise everyone as Lefthanded Ice-Cream Spatula Salesmen or something, sneak aboard the enemy flagship while in flight during general quarters, waltz into the bridge or wherever the McGuffin is, get past all guards and alarms and killer robots, discombobulate the McGuffin, and then the Republican Fleet can escape through hyperspace without being tracked, and you will be left behind to be captured and executed. Go to it!

Then when comedy relief robot Fussy Butler points out that the Dogcatcher should clear any espionage plans with his Commanding Officer, Hotshot Dogcatcher tells him to shut up. And he does! Some robot.

The Republic has no chain of command! No discipline! No military ranks! People just kind of do stuff whenever they feel like it! Because nothing matters.

Honestly, at his point, had I been Token Stormtrooper, I would have been begging Team Empire to take me back, except for the fact that their chain of command and military discipline operates in the exact same way: everyone disobeys orders and shoots underlings who disobey orders and forgets, one scene later, who mutinied against whom. The sole difference is that the Resistance soldiers shoot mutineers with non-lethal stun-guns and zoink them with cattleprods. The film-perpetrator has never met, talked to, nor heard rumors of anyone serving in any military ever, nor ever seen a John Wayne flick.

Then, more stupid happens.

5

NON-PLOT B: MARY SUE AND MASTER MOPEY

A h! But you were wondering about the B plot, were you not?

Remember how the whole last movie was spent looking for the star map that Luke Skywalker left behind to allow his old friends to find him? Because he wanted the galaxy to call upon him again when the need for the Jedi arose once more?

Remember how Mary Sue found Luke's father's lightsaber, touched it, and had a mysterious, mystical vision sent by The Force, showing her the way here?

Remember her walking up to Master Luke, the Last Jedi, and holding out his father's lightsaber, offering it to him, that he might take up his weapon, come to help his sister, and restore hope to the fight, and peace to the galaxy?

You don't remember? Well, neither did the film-perpetrator here. There is no B Plot. Nothing comes of anything and nothing makes sense.

Non-plot B starts with the Last Jedi plucking the proffered lightsaber from Mary Sue and tossing it contemptuously over his shoulder off a cliff. He then contemptuously asked her what the heck she is doing here. (Not to worry: members of the audience, bored and uncomfortable in their seats in nearly empty theaters, are each wondering the self-same thing.)

The blind cutpurse who pilfers the bag and leaves the coins now strikes again. The film-perpetrator is trying to copy the scene in *Empire Strikes Back* where Yoda the Jedi Master is introduced. At first, Yoda seems senile, crass, rude, and silly, but it is act, a put-on, meant to test the would-be student to see if he is faithful, sincere, and humble enough to be an apprentice. It is time-tested, tried-and-true shtick from martial arts movies.

Here, Mopey actually is senile, crass, rude, and silly, and it is not an act.

(Not to worry. Mary Sue soon proves not to be faithful, sincere, or humble. Between breaking down his door with a wookie, and beating his head with a stick, she is hardly the image of an obedient disciple.)

His motivation is that he is despondent to the point of psychological instability, and he wants to die. He has lost all hope, surrendered to all despair, regards Jedi-knighthood as pointless, if not evil, and wants the Jedi order to die with him.

In the same way I cannot call the bitter old ruined hag in this filthy movie leading the Resistance by the name Leia, I cannot in good conscience refer to this deliberate and nasty mockery of Luke by the name of the real character: here-after, let him be called Mopey Sulkwalker.

(My heart goes out in pity to Mark Hamill, who was bound by contract to portray the character a sick-minded film-perp forced on him. There are not enough four-letter words in the entire Anglo-Saxon language to express the disgust and rage any honest fan must feel at this malign desecration of one of the, if not *the*, fan-favorite sci-fi hero of all time and space. Only Russians can cuss such cusses.)

Mary Sue pesters Mopey while he milks an obscenely bloated green-milk-giving Dr. Seuss sea-cow, dribbles green milk in his beard, she nags him while he fishes with the stupidest fish-spear ever imagined in this or any other galaxy, and she harasses and importunes him while he sulks many a sulking sulk.

This goes on and on for what is surely a geologic age, unless it is an era, epoch, or eon.

Then a scene happens where she has a vision of Emo Wanker, pasty-faced punk, standing in the room with her, and meanwhile he is having a vision of her. This could have been a cool idea, but the film-perp decides to play it for laughs. Emo tries to mind control her, but it does not work, and she tries to shoot him, and that also does not work, but instead blows a hole in the wall, nearly-killing two comedy-relief alien dwarf frog nuns who are wandering aimlessly around the set for no reason.

(Nothing comes of their comedy-relief near-deaths either, by the way. The alien dwarf frog police do not come by, nor does the father of the nearly-killed alien dwarf frog nun politely ask Mopey to drive the maniacal blaster-happy Mary Sue away from the sacred Jedi shrine where people are living. Like everything in the non-plot, the alien dwarfs of Mopey Island are an element that could have been removed entirely without any need to change to anything else in the film.)

Later, Mary Sue has a vision of Emo coming out of the shower with his shirt off, so she can be embarrassed yet romantically attracted to his pasty-pale body and chinless wimp-face. Comedy! Or not.

Then a scene happens where Mary Sue attacks Mopey

the Jedi Master with a lightsaber. Without getting wounded, or breaking a sweat, she easily yet effortlessly curb-stomps him. Because he is a punk. He is knocked on his ass after one exchange of strikes and parries, with her sword tip in his face, while he cowers.

Keep in mind that the events of this film and the prior film together are, at most, a week to ten days long. Keep in mind that at the beginning of the prior film, Mary Sue did not believe that the Force existed at all. She thought Luke Skywalker was a myth, merely a story, as were all Jedi. So here she is a week later, with no training either in the Force, or in fencing, or in fighting, cleaning the clock of the foremost Jedi warrior of the galaxy.

Or maybe that scene came earlier or later. It does not matter, since these scenes could have been portrayed in any order. They are not connected to each other. One, both, or all could have been cut out entirely without changing the—I cannot call it a plot—without changing the dreary repetition of meaningless, silly, depressing, or stupid events. Nothing matters.

Then a scene happens where Mopey agrees to train her, and to teach her three lessons. THREE LESSONS! Remember that number. The film-perp took the trouble to mention that number, so you should remember it.

In the first lesson he tells her to reach out. She closes her eyes stretches out her hand, because she is an idiot and thinks he meant it literally. He playfully tickles the hand with a grass blade, and when she, awe in her voice, asks if that is the Force tickling her, he says yes, and then slaps her sharply across the knuckles with a stick.

This amused me because it caused her pain, and I hate her.

But the scene made no sense and was not in character

either for Mopey or Luke or Mary Sue or anyone. This girl has already, at this point, used the Force to dominate a stormtrooper's brain, to fight a lightsaber battle against a trained swordsman, and telepathically to send and to receive visions across interstellar distances. So, this bit was just plain stupid. I cannot tell if it was supposed to be funny, or supposed to show that Mopey is the worst teacher ever, or to show that Mary Sue is a moron. Not to worry, though. Nothing comes of it.

Then Mary Sue senses the circle of life, and Mopey tells her that the Force does not require the Jedi, and will continue to exist without them. While being true, it is an utterly meaningless statement because no one ever said the opposite was true. It is not a point anyone is curious about.

It is like saying plants will grow without farmers. It is a true statement, but who wants a field of weeds and kudzu rather than a field of wheat? Who wants cities to starve?

It is an utterly stupid statement because someone seeking Jedi training is seeking the discipline needed to control these mysterious powers, and to learn how to fight the Sith and other evildoers.

I honestly do not remember if it is at this point, or earlier, or later, that Mopey blames the Jedi for the Fall of the Republic which Luke heroically and successfully restored.

His logic is that since Mace Windu could not stop Emperor Palpatine the Sith's usurpation of power, therefore, QED, Mopey should stand by with his hands in his pockets, moping, while Supreme Leader Snoopy conquers the galaxy, kills Mopey's family, tortures, kills, rapes, and loots whole planets.

How the past failure of one's predecessors to overcome the evil they opposed robs one of the moral authority needed to oppose present evil is a bit of moral calculus whose intricacy escapes me.

Please note that this plot point could have been dropped into this scene, or earlier, or later, or been left out entirely without requiring any other change to any other scene, because it affects nothing else in the film.

Please note that this so-called lesson did not actually teach anyone anything.

Then Mary Sue discovers Master Mopey has cut himself off from the Force! Which I think means he is dead, and he cannot use Force powers any more, but he uses them again in short order, since reconnecting is apparently a matter of a moment's concentration. So, this makes no sense either metaphorically or literally.

What about the second and third lesson? Well, there are none. The film-perp forgot. Nothing matters.

And it is never clear why she needs training to begin with: she can do all the Force-tricks anyone else can do, and better than anyone, with the sole exception of Snoopy.

Mary Sue has a vision, senses the existence of the Dark Side, and Mopey throws an absurd hissy-fit, claiming that she should be afraid of the Dark Side: But she looked toward the Dark Side with no change of expression. (In fact, she never changes expression at any point throughout the movie.)

He then says that he was wrong not to be afraid when he sensed the Dark Side previously, namely, when he sensed it inside Emo and thought he could lead the boy back to the Sunny Side.

Ponder a moment how utterly out of character for a Star Wars Jedi this comment is. The Dark Side are the side who give into fear. Recall that Yoda objected to Anakin being trained at all, despite his natural strength in the Force, because there was "much fear in him" i.e. making the child too vulnerable to the Dark Side. The Good Guys are the able to use the Force in benevolent ways because and only because they never give into fear. This stated explicitly in several prior movies. But nothing matters.

Then a scene happens where Mary Sue seeks out the Dark Side, which lives in an underground lake next to a magic mirror. She plunges into the water. She can swim, even though she was raised on a sand planet with no open water.

Then comes a long scene of her having a psychedelic vision of an infinite number of reflections of herself. She breaks out of this illusion by reminding herself that as a perfect Mary Sue, or maybe the boy from Dr. Seuss' *Happy Birthday to You*, since she can call out "I am I!" and emotionally validate her own self-esteem to herself.

She conjures the Force to bring her a vision of who her parents are. Two shadows approach through foggy mirror. They get closer, *closer*, CLOSER!

But the image fades and she is just staring at her own stupid, blank, acting-free face in the mirror, showing the same blank expression she wears throughout this purgatory of a film experience, and her own voice comes on as a voice-over, confirming that she will never get any answers. Nothing matters.

And why does the character have a first-person voice-over talking to the audience at that one time, in that one scene, and at no other time in the film? It was awkward and jarring. It would have reminded the audience that we were merely watching a movie, if this had been a movie, instead of a flaming rubbish heap.

6

NON-PLOT A (CONT): DIM AND DANK
ON PLANET SWANK

Tweedledim and Tweedledank to go to planet Swank. Ponder, for a moment, the magnitude of unadulterated *dumb* this entails.

Allegedly, these are two officers of the last dwindling remnant of the sole remaining flotilla of the once-great Space Navy of the Galactic Republic. The flotilla consists of one cruiser and maybe six or seven small ships or spaceboats. They are desperately low on fuel. Whenever they jump through hyperspace, the enemy materializes behind them, maintaining the hot pursuit. Long-range gun fire from the pursuit is picking off the ships one by one.

And one spaceboat with plenty of fuel suddenly departs from the flotilla, dances tra-la away from the pursuit, easily outdistances it, flies hither and yon through the galaxy without being tracked or pursued, and lands on planet Swank.

If this was the special invisible rocketship of Space Ghost, I did not hear the line which gave that explanation. If Dogcatcher suddenly had authority to order all the remaining ephahs of dilithium crystal fuel-bars into the

Phantom Cruiser, likewise, I did not hear it. If the planet Swank, by cosmic coincidence, just so happened to be along their line of flight, likewise. The reason why the idiotic Resistance did not all, then and there, climb into smaller ships and all follow Tweedledim to planet Swank, likewise.

Dim and Dank park their starship on the beach (while an offscreen comedy relief voice tells them not to park there) and they walk into the casino, which is running full blast and full of fun during the Civil War. With Dim and Dank is Annoying Robot Billiard Ball, the failed knock-off of R2-D2. He is there, even though he belongs to Hotshot and in fact is his copilot. Merciless comedy is committed when a drunk alien mistakes Billiard Ball for a slot machine and shoves gold coins into his dashboard lighter slot.

Then, with a tin-eared change of pace and mood, in the next second, Dim the Stormtrooper is gushing over how pretty and wonderful the casino is, how pretty the dresses and such, while Cattleprod Rose is virtue signaling as hard and fast as her virtue can signal: she declares, for no reason and based on nothing, that all these people here are arms manufacturers, who got rich manufacturing arms for the Empire. Arms manufacturers are bad! Rich people are bad! BAD!

Also, the home planet where she and her dead sister were raised was raided and stripped of resources by the Empire. Which makes no sense, if the Empire was destroyed and the First Order is a small band of rebels trying to restore imperial rule. Maybe she says something about the Empire stealing her pony when she was a child. There is a racetrack next to the casino, and we see a mean man beating a space racehorse.

Tweedledim and Tweedledank see the Master Codebreaker wearing the puce carnation in his lapel from across the room.

Do you remember the EIGHTEEN-HOUR time limit mentioned, and then repeated, which will hem in the possible time during which the Rebel flotilla has its sole and slender hope of escaping from the overwhelming power of the Imperial Deathfleet? Yes?

Well, your memory cells were wasted, because that time limit never comes up again. Instead you should have remembered something that slid by during a medium-range pan of the establishing shot, when a comedy relief voice from offstage told Dim and Dank that they could not park on the beach. THAT turns out to be a crucial plot point.

Because, before the Tweedle twins, ace secret agents, can approach the Master Codebreaker, uniformed thugs pop up. No, these are not Imperial Stormtroopers, nor the Praetorian Guard, nor even the elite SWAT team of Outer Space. They are the traffic cops of Planet Swank, who are mad that the Tweedle twins left their spaceship double parked. The meter maids.

So, the traffic cops approach these two, whom the cops think are wealthy patrons of the casino, and tell them to move their vehicle. One of the Tweedles goes to move the spaceship to the proper boating slip without any further ado, and meanwhile the other approaches the Master Codebreaker and hires him.

Oh, no. *That* does not happen. That would make *sense*.

Instead, the traffic cops do not realize they are messing with an ex-Imperial Stormtrooper, raised and conditioned since before birth to be the deadliest killing machine in the galaxy, and before they can blink, he cleans their clocks with his expert military... oh, no, wait.

That also does not happen. That also would make sense.

Instead, the traffic cops are suddenly confronted with the Wrench Monkey, who can throw grown men across the room with her zoink-powered cattleprod. She begins zoinking and flattening these mooks with the same ease she zoinked the Token Stormtrooper Tweedledim in the first reel, because... oh, no, wait.

That would perhaps not make sense, but it would be in step with what happened earlier.

Instead, while the traffic cops beat down Dank the Wrench Monkey with their atomic nightsticks, Token Stormtrooper Tweedledim, hands in pockets, whistling tunelessly, wanders over to the baccarat tables, and picks up a martini from a passing cocktail waitress, flirts with a debutante with a low-cut decolletage, generally blends into the crowd, and thereby escapes clean away from the Rebellion and their idiot leadership, which is what he was trying to do in the first scene where we met him.

Again, this at least would be in step with what happened earlier.

But no. No, no. Instead the rocket-powered stupidity hammer, now getting a boost from jet-assist take-off tubes, zooms out of the screen and clocks me in the skull, rolling a natural twenty so I take double damage.

The traffic cops take down the moron twins in one frame of the film without breaking a sweat, in yet another one-and-done fight scene, executed with no zest, no wit, and no interest.

Dim and Dank are in jail.

They are not in prison uniforms, not in sexually segregated male and female jail cells, and no one thought to impound the Billiard Ball that was with them.

They still have their belts, bootlaces, and neckties. I

guess no one cares whether prisoners hang themselves in this universe. More likely the audience members will.

Maybe this is supposed to be the private holding cell of the casino owner, who merely locks up drunks and sore losers as whim strikes him. Admittedly, that makes no sense.

But neither does anything else.

Then more stupid happens.

7

NON-PLOT B (CONT): EMO, MOPEY AND THE SAD BACKSTORY

Meanwhile, back on Mopey Island on planet Ahch-To (gesundheit!), there is almost a hint of an interesting plot as Mary Sue discovers the sad, sad, ever so sad backstory of Master Mopey and Emo Wanker. It is a tragedy so deep that Mopey cannot bring himself to talk about it! She has to threaten to cut off his head before he opens up!

Get out your crying bags! Tears will flow!

Mary Sue hears Mopey's side of the story first. It seems Mopey was the grandmaster running the Jedi Academy. He was training Emo, the son of his sister and of his best friend, but then Emo turned absolutely and irredeemably evil for no reason, recruited or killed the other students, and burned down the school. In flashback, we see Mopey is a punk, so Emo easily blasts him through the roof of the dorm with one hand.

Then she hears Emo's side of the story! Mopey came into the dorm after midnight with a drawn lightsaber to kill the teen wanker as he slept. In flashback, we see Mopey is a punk, so Emo easily parries him in his sleep and blasts him through the roof of the dorm with one hand.

Then she hears the second version of Mopey's side of the story! Mopey came into the dorm after midnight with a drawn lightsaber to kill teen Emo as he slept. But he did not really and truly mean to kill him, drawing the lightsaber was just an instinctive reflex, because Mopey is a trigger-happy jerk whose first instinct is to kill his teenaged nephew in his sleep. In flashback, we see Mopey is a punk, so Emo easily parries him in his sleep and blasts him through the roof of the dorm with one hand. (Good to know that this part of the story, Mopey being a weak-ass punk, is consistent in all three tellings.) Emo is a moron, and so does not confirm that Mopey is dead, but leaves him buried under the rubble.

Please note that the backstory explains nothing. Emo turned absolutely and irredeemably evil for no reason because Supreme Leader Snoopy turned him to the Dumb Side. Who is Supreme Leader Snoopy? How did he meet Emo Vader? What convinced him to join the Sith, who had been utterly defeated in the first trilogy? What happened to the other Jedi Academy students who left with Emo, and became his own personal cadre of evil knights with space wizard powers?

No answers. No backstory. Nothing makes sense.

When Mary Sue learns these boring revelations, she does not change her mind, since she did not have anything on her mind to begin with. Nor does she change her expression.

Remember I said tears would flow? Well, that is like the three lessons in being a Jedi, or the eighteen hour time limit before the Rebel flotilla is destroyed. Another unkept promise. Unless, of course, you are crying for the same reason I am, at the missed opportunities and lost potential of writing an ever-lovin' STAR WARS MOVIE with cotton-pickin'

MARK HAMILL in it, reprising his iconic role, and how easy it would have been to have a plot.

It is not all that hard to come up with an interesting back story. How about this?

Snoke is actually Darth Plagueis, the master of Darth Sidious, a Sith Lord briefly mentioned in a prior episode, the one who learned the secret of immortality. His body is rotting because he is a living mummy, kept in a state of semi-animation by an unnatural perversion of the Force impregnating his every bloodcell and forcing it into a hideous mockery of life.

He is immensely more powerful than any other Sith Lord who has gone before, and can hypnotize whole planets' worth of people and turn their hearts to the Dark Side, which is how he eroded the power of the Republic so quickly and made the common people yearn for a return of the glory days of the Empire.

Luke, sensing this growing shadow from afar, and realizing that Darth Plagueis could kill him with a thought across interstellar distances, retreated to the hidden Jedi monastery, whose holy ground protects him. Luke is frantically seeking through the ancient books and scrolls for some clue as to how to hinder this monstrous evil. Darth Plagueis easily can corrupt any Jedi apprentice Luke attempts to train, including his own nephew, because anyone trained to be sensitive to the Force is, at least at first, vulnerable to subtle influences. But Luke has cut himself off from the Force to hide all trace of himself from the Sith Overlord's malignant and nigh-omniscient influence. (And, just to tie up lose threads, there is no McGuffin space radar tracking the Rebel flotilla through hyperspace: that is merely the side effect of the Sith Overlord's clairvoyant vision.)

He is thousands of years old. Like the Kenobis, the Skywalkers are all descended from Snoke, for they are a bloodline deliberately bred by him over the centuries to be Force-sensitive: the final child of this age-long breeding program was originally meant to be Darth Vader, but on his deathbed, Vader turned to the Light Side and so escaped his fate.

Who is the second candidate? The death of Vader forced Darth Plagueis out of hiding. He had to create the next candidate. It is not Kylo. Kylo is strong in the Force, but too imperfect to house Snoke and all Snoke's power.

The second candidate is Rey, or, rather, her as-yet unborn son. She will be impregnated against her will, and the baby from birth will be possessed by Snoke's mind and spirit, as Snoke needs this child's flesh as the housing in which his unclean spirit shall dwell forever more.

The reason why Rey is so powerful in the Force is that she is the end product of Snoke's secret breeding program. The whole commotion of the First Order and the Resistance was nothing but a distraction meant to provoke the Force into locating her and bringing her forth on the galactic stage, as someone to be the equal and opposite of Kylo.

As for ruling the galaxy, that means nothing to the immortal being: he will let Kylo be Emperor for all his life, a span of time that, to Snoke, is like a single afternoon. Rey will be Empress and will be the mother of the Dark Messiah.

Her only choice is whether the marry Kylo Ren, or to be impregnated directly by Snoke's brain, using the warped life-energies of the Force to create life in her womb, just as her grandmother

Shmi Skywalker was impregnated.

Unbeknownst to Anakin, his mother Shmi gave birth to

a young sister, Rey's mom, Anarey, while abducted by the Sand People of Tatooine. Anarey was sold to the cousin tribe of Sand People on Jakku, and lived as a slave, until she was saved by Drokko Kira the crimelord, secretly Lord Kira of the Royal House of Onderon, the deadly Planet of Beasts, in exile. Drokko, after a stormy courtship, weds Anarey. Police, rival crimelords, royal assassins sent by Drokko's evil twin brother, the usurper Dralk, were all hunting Drokko, and forced him to flee.

He hid wife and daughter on the Sand Planet for safe-keeping, promising to return: but Anarey is abducted by the Sith Lady Maleficent, who is seeking her genetically perfect child for Lord Snoke. Anarey, weeping, hides her daughter with the poor but honest junk dealer Deela Jettster, sister of Dexter. Lord Kira returns in the third movie, horribly maimed but rebuilt with cyborg limbs, a remorseless killing machine, and recruits Rey to go to the forbidden Sith Home-world, Moraband, to mount a hopeless rescue of her mother.

Is that too much backstory? Okay, so we do not need to explain about Drokko Kira the crimelord and his beautiful wife Anarey, the sister of Anakin. Skip that part.

Maybe not the greatest story in the universe, sure: but at least this would have been *something*. It would at least *try* to keep audience interest.

If, at about this time, you get the impression that the film-perp spent a zillion dollars of Disney's money just to indulge in the sick joke of seeing how long he could get away with mocking the audience, teasing us into thinking he would, any scene now, begin to tell a proper story and then, instead of a story, twisted our noses, and scrawled obscene graffiti over the faces of our beloved heroes and heroines, then your suspicions are the same as mine.

Now, that is a plot idea I offered above I simply threw together while I was sitting here typing this.

I am sure it can use polish, and that it might sound a bit like *Dune* or *First Lensman*. So what? I am using it as an example of when a plot reveal reveals something interesting, something that adds to the drama and does not subtract from it. It is not just a pie in the face of the chump audience, while the movie-perp who fooled us into expecting a real story utters a donkey laugh.

There was no real story. Let me return to describing it, or, rather, autopsying it.

I forgot so say that Chewbacca and R2D2 are also there on Mopey Island. They did not need to be there, of course, since nothing comes of them, and the plot does not use them.

Chewie kills and eats one of the cutie-pie comedy-relief bunny-penguins that infest the island. These are toyetic critters, no doubt shoved into the film to help with toy sales. Again, whether the scene was meant to be morbidly funny, or just to demean Chewie's character, or just to be stupid and insult the viewers, no mortal can say. You will have to inquire in the dark inferno where the hell-being dwells who inspired the film-perp to pen this dreck to discover the answer, I suppose.

R2D2 has the only good scene, and the only good line, in the film. And he does not even speak it. When Mopey Sulk-walker fondly greets him, for a moment, like Gollum almost becoming Smeagol once more, Mopey almost becomes Luke.

The old man bitterly asks if the brave and chipper little robot is going to say anything to persuade him? Without any ado, the robot turns on his hologram projector, and plays the clip of the young Princess Leia, Luke's sister, asking Obi-Wan Kenobi for help.

That was actually a touching scene. It made me want to see a Star Wars sequel some day.

Nothing comes of it. Sulkwalker just utters a curse and slinks away, sulking.

Meanwhile, back on Lord Snoopy's ship, Lord Snoopy browbeats Emo Vader by (quite truthfully) telling him he is a weak-willed punk wearing a dumb black mask, and (quite truthfully) telling him that he is a sissy and a softie, because he let a young girl who cannot change expression kick his butt.

Emo has another hissy-fit in the elevator, and we are treated to a minute or so (but it seemed like years) of watching this whining, baby-faced, blubbering moron weeping and smashing his helmet into the elevator wall in helpless rage. Some people cannot get over the fact that Trump won.

Since this is the fourth or fifth screaming tantrum we have seen from this character, I did not at first realize that the film-perpetrator seriously intended this scene to have a serious point. It was supposed to be a head-fake, a red herring, where we see Kylo smash his mask to bits, and conclude that he has given up on his hero-worship of Darth Vader, hence has made an about-face to the Sunny Side. But he has not. He is still evil. Only now, he is evil without a mask.

Well, the head fake did not work on me, because this scene of Emo going totally emo, hulking out, losing it, banshee-screaming, and smashing things did not appear any different from any other of his emo scenes. I assumed he could find and don another mask if he really wanted. I assume he had a dozen of them stacked in his sock drawer.

The problem with this scene is that when Snoopy calls Emo's mask silly, everyone in the audience suddenly realizes that he is right, and the mask actually *is* silly, and that there is no way any character would actually wear it: there is no in-story reason for such a thing.

The real Vader wore a mask because his head was horribly scarred, and he needed medical apparatus permanently applied to his face. Taking off his mask hastened his death, but also showed he was finally freed of the darkness that dominated his destiny.

In this case, young Vader-fanboy is wearing a mask he thinks is intimidating, but it is not. He is someone who never wins a single fight. Everyone in the audience suddenly remembers that they are sitting in chairs in a theater, watching a boring, poorly-done, and malign dumpster-fire of a film.

The real Vader could dress as he darned well pleased, because he was an aristocrat and a badass, who loomed over everyone in the movie and Force-choked anyone who back-talked him. Emo Vader is an angst-ridden, emotional, whining teen who whines emotionally. And he is someone who never wins a single fight.

I think Emo flies off to go shoot at his Mom at this point, or perhaps that scene comes earlier or later, because who cares? No scene is actually connected in any order to any scene. Like every other scene in this plotless mess, the elevator mask-smashing scene could have been deleted in its entirety with no change to any other scene.

For no particular reason, back on Mopey island, Mary Sue decides that Emo Vader is an angst-ridden, emotional, whining teen who whines emotionally, and therefore she can turn him to the Sunny Side.

Mopey kicks her in the buttocks and tells her to go on

this suicide mission and die, as this will decrease the count of living Jedi in the galaxy to zero, and ensure the victory of the Sith, which is apparently his goal.

Oh, no, wait, that would be in keeping with what had gone before.

No, rather, he tells her not to go, and the film-perp trolls the audience by having the same lines lifted from the parallel scene in *Return of the Jedi* where Luke is warned by his Jedi Master that there is no hope of goodness left in Vader.

Except in that film, Luke was tempted and Vader did turn and kill his master, whereas in this one, Mary Sue cannot be tempted, and Emo does not turn.

Here is what happens instead: Mary Sue leaves. Mopey Sulkwalker goes to the sacred tree housing the ancient and irreplaceable library of the Jedi, which consists of five books, and for no reason decides to burn it all. He changes his mind for no reason at the last moment, but then the ghost of Yoda for no reason shows up, a new Force Power no one ever had before shows up for no reason, Yoda calls down lighting from a clear blue sky for no reason, and burns up the sacred tree. Mopey has to jump and stumble out of the way of the blast that otherwise would kill him.

Yoda remarks that it is indeed time for the Jedi to end. As for the sacred books, he says "Page-turners, they were not. Yes, yes, yes. Wisdom, they held, but that library contained nothing that the girl Rey does not already possess."

Get that? The teacher of Ben Kenobi and Luke Skywalker dismisses and burns the sacred books of the Jedi in an act of pointless vandalism, because Mary Sue is so wise she does not need them.

Then, Yoda pokes him with a stick. "Ah, Skywalker...still

looking to the horizon. Never here! Now, hmm? The need in front of your nose!" Which, since this is the one lesson Luke spent all that time on the Swamp Planet learning, it is yet another example of setting at naught all growth, triumph, and accomplishment of all characters in all prior films.

Meanwhile, Mary Sue flies the Millennium Falcon to within a mile of Snoopy's superdreadnought, she lets down her hair, applies lipstick and launches herself in an escape pod into space toward the enemy ship.

Immediately the radar crew and crack-shot gunnery officers, doing their job in a professional fashion, recognize that anything dropped from an unknown ship might be a bomb, and blow her escape pod to smithereens, and then burn the expanding ash clouds into ionized dust with a fan of high-energy radiation beams.

No, wait, that would have made sense. Instead, Mary Sue is recovered, arrested, and then loaded down with forty pounds of chains, injected with sodium pentothal, interrogated, lasered to death, and her skull is now an ashtray in the Sith Lord's smoking parlor.

No, wait, that would have followed from what had gone before. Mary Sue is arrested, and put in handcuffs, but then taken out of handcuffs, and she has an audience with Lord Snoopy.

Here follows the one and only comedy bit in the whole film I actually thought funny.

Mary Sue attempts to levitate her lightsaber to her hand. Lord Snoopy flicks the flying weapon telekinetically, so it swoops past Mary's outstretched fingers, circles behind her and then smartly clocks Mary Sue on the back of her empty skull as it flies on wires across the room and back to Snoopy's desk.

I laughed out loud, first, because Mary Sue actually

changed her empty expression, or almost, and, second, because being hit in the head caused her pain and I hate her.

Then Lord Snoopy utters the one and only line in the film that actually was a good line spoken aloud. The bright moment in this entire slog through the slough of despond known as *Last Jedi* is when the Sith Master reveals that he is the one who bridged the minds of Emo Vader and Mary Sue.

"I stoked Ren's conflicted soul. I knew he was not strong enough to hide from you. And you were not wise enough to resist the bait."

He's weak and she's stupid. Sounds exactly right. What does it tell you about a film, if the only true thing said in the whole running time is uttered by the bad guy?

Lord Snoopy then demands to know the location of Mopey, and Mary Sue defies him. He laughs and reveals that since he is the one who reached her mind on the Mopey Island, he of course knows exactly where it is.

No, sorry, that would have made sense.

Lord Snoopy then demands to know the location of Mopey, and he sucks the information easily out of Mary Sue's untrained mind, and orders the rebuilt Death Star to blast the Mopey Island planet to bits, which it immediately does, killing Mopey instantly. Only the obscenely bloated green-milk giving sea-cow is seen floating among the rubble of outerspace, hooting mournfully. Mary Sue is then lasered to death and her skull is now an ashtray in the Sith Lord's smoking parlor.

No, sorry, that was just wishful thinking.

Lord Snoopy then demands to know the location of Mopey, and Mary Sue tells him without hesitation, because Mopey said he wanted to die: stormtroopers land and kill

Mopey while he is milking an obscenely bloated green-milk giving Dr. Seuss sea-cow. The sea-cow rears up, snorting and roaring, then reveals herself to be the master Jedi, Umglark the Great, Yoda's tutor, and Force-chokes the stormtroopers to death with her mind-powers, before psychokinetically causing the superatomic engines of the battleship in orbit overhead to melt down and overload, wiping out the entire expedition in an expanding fireball of her wrath.

We see the blue-lined ghost of Mopey Sulkwalker being kicked in the butt, over and over again, by the blue-lined ghosts of his father and prior teachers as he is led off to Jedi afterlife. Roll credits.

No, sorry, that would have followed from what came before.

What actually happens is that Snoopy sees Mopey is retired, hence no threat, Mary Sue is untrained, hence no threat, and Emo is an idiot. Snoopy summarily orders her death, which makes sense, but orders Emo to do it, which makes no sense.

At this point, what is his plan? What is his long-term goal? Get them? Mug the rebels? That was the whole plan?

Then more stupid happens. Unrelentingly.

8

NON-PLOT A (CONT): SPACEHORSES
AND CODEBREAKERS

Ready for more pain? Let the space camera of your imagination zoom back to planet Swank, where Token Stormtrooper Tweedledim and Zoink-powered Wrench Monkey Tweedledank are locked into the least secure jail in the galaxy.

While in jail, Dim and Dank in loud voices discuss their secret mission as secret members of the secret Resistance, thereby waking up the Master Codebeaker, who happens to also be under arrest and sleeping in the same cell.

Dim and Dank, like expert spies and secret agents that they are, blow off the fellow without finding out who he is.

This is not the same Master Codebreaker they saw wearing a carnation at the baccarat tables, but he *says* he is a Master Codebreaker, and that they can trust him. Either he is telling the truth or his is lying. Either way, this plot twist is idiotic.

If he is telling the truth, the bartender who sent them on this mission, looking for one and only one person on this planet, is an idiot because trustworthy Master Code-breakers are apparently as common as locksmiths or space-electricians. If he is not, they are idiots for believing him.

I need not bother making up an insulting nickname for this guy, and that for two reasons:

First, he already has a dumb nickname. It is "Don't Join" or DJ for short. I am not making this up! DJ is the dumb actual dumb name of this dumb character. He is not a disc jockey. It stands for "Don't Join"—a dumb sentiment.

Second, he actually is a character, which is to say, he is a pretend person, who has a series of character traits and sticks to them, unlike everyone else.

I have more respect for DJ than anyone else in the film. He almost seems one-dimensional to me, even though he has but a bit part. The main characters are zero-dimensional, like clumsy and soulless meat puppets.

DJ strolls grandly out of the jailcell by hacking the electronic lock without breaking stride, flipping open all the other jail cells as he goes. Dim and Dank, eyes bugged out in comic surprise, flop out of the jail cell behind him, calling toward his retreating back while he ignores them.

But then the traffic cops of Planet Swank are hot on their tails!

And we all know these cops, and indeed, the whole planet, are completely inconsequential to the main conflict in their story, and so therefore (by the rules of laughably bad writing this film-perp follows) the traffic cops of Swank get more screen time and are a bigger threat than Captain Phasmid and all her stormtroopers.

So then Annoying Robot Billiard Ball in an unfunny comedy relief bit, pops up to fight the traffic cops!

The plucky little bot shoots them, not with bullets nor bolts of energy, but by spitting out all the coins the drunk alien stuck into his dashboard lighter slot thinking he was a slot machine. Good thing Annoying Robot Billiard Ball had a coin-spitting mechanism especially installed for just that purpose!

The coins are flung with such force by the basketball-shaped machine-sidekick that the traffic cops are battered into unconsciousness with multiple skull fractures and brain contusions, and also, they slip and pratfall comically on the spinning coin piles underfoot!

I estimate at least ninety-one firkins of coinage are spilled over the floor, equal to eleventy-four hundred Polish Zlotys, or a dozen-score and a half troy-weight strips of gold-pressed latinum.

This raises three questions: first, if the robot maker decided to install a man-killing coin-shooter into his dumb-bots, why not install a snub-nosed blastergun? Second, if one undersized dumb-bot armed with a coin-shooter can outmatch two braces of gun-toting veteran traffic cops in armor, why not replace all the cops on the planet with dumb-bots? Third, instead of shooting it at cops, why not use the money to buy fuel for the Resistance flotilla that was running out of gas, and shoot something ELSE at the cops, like buttons, or salad forks, or even ever-lovin' bullets, fer Forcesake?

For that matter, why not simply pay the freakin' parking ticket with the gold coins, and have the traffic cops thank them with a smile? The cops are not the bad guys in this film. The stormtroopers are.

Or maybe I am wrong about that. Perhaps the film-perp is with Team Empire, and wants us to think Team Resistance are the bad guys.

I note that the Empire does not commit any atrocities or unlawful acts while on screen, at least, not in this film. Indeed, the only unlawful act which appears on screen is when members of the Resistance, apparently out of sheer malice against the well-to-do, unleash a stampede of space-racehorses into a casino, an act of murderous and reckless vandalism.

No nursemaids with babe in arms are shown being trampled to death by the stampede, nor the waitresses nor charwomen, but it is safe to assume this happened. Elderly drunks and women in evening gowns are not known for any particular ability to ninja-backflip out of the way of a raging stampede.

In my heart of hearts, of course, I firmly believe the very Master Codebreaker the Tweedle twins were sent here to find indeed died moaning in broken horror, bones askew and body smashed to jelly, under the remorseless hooves of the deadly herd the two unleashed. With him died the only hope of the Resistance for salvation.

But even if, as it could not be, no people were maimed or killed, the property damage to the casino is immense. If this had been, as it easily could have been, established in the story to be the exclusive nightclub patronized only by Party members and ranking officers in the Empire, the vandalism would have been against a legitimate military target. But, no. These were civilians. We discover in the very next scene (see below) that they included manufacturers helping to supply the Rebellion, making arms and equipment for them.

So, this would be like someone wandering into Monaco during World War Two, finding a nightclub where he thinks men from the Krupp armament company are gambling with Italian fascists and German Nazis, and unleashing a stampede to trample them and their wives, bartenders, band-members, waiters, croupiers, and dancing girls, but lo and behold, instead it is men from Ford and Colt, Sikorsky and

Grumman, and the industrialists and arms manufacturers on our side.

Back up. I skipped a scene. I should have mentioned that the Tweedles, Dank and Dim, released the space-racehorses from their space-barn when they were trying to hide there. A paltry but honest slave boy named Oliver Twist is the space groom there, where he spends his morning and evenings being beaten savagely by his evil space master, Simon Legree. Oliver sees Dank and Dim hiding, and his paltry but honest slave boy finger creeps weakly toward the alarm button to summon the police, but suddenly Twee-dledank, the dumpy zoink-dwarf, leaps on him and zoinks him with her cattleprod.

No, wait, that is not quite right. She only zoinks black spacemen.

She shows Oliver her secret decoder ring that proves she is one of the agents of The Shadow, secret fighter for justice, and this so inspires Oliver with hope and goodness that he gives them leave to go. Instead of taking him with, they leave him in his miserable bondage, just like Anakin Skywalker's Mom was left, but liberate the space-horses. Simon Legree returns, finds a zillion gold-pressed latinum bar's worth of thoroughbreds missing, and beats the boy savagely. Unless he does not. I do not remember clearly, since it was roughly this point when I started fast-forwarding past scenes that looked too stupid to watch, which was nearly all of them.

Then comes a boring chase scene on spacehorseback I won't describe, except to say that when horsemen are being chased by aviators in flying machines, the smart money is on the flying machines. Or would be, in a film that was not relentlessly stupid. They get away. Except not really.

Of course, Dank the Zoink Dwarf is the rider guiding the horse and Dim is the baggage clinging to the horse's rump. Because he is black, and no black man in this movie is ever shown doing anything competent. On the other hand, no one of any race or either sex is shown doing anything competent, so don't read anything sinister into this.

Dank the Zoink Dwarf, I should mention, was born and raised on a mining planet as a poverty-racked coal miner's daughter, and so of course is an expert equestrienne. Girls in this film simply get to do things, like be admirals or be Jedi, shoot vehicle-mounted weapons and ride space-horses, without any training or aptitude.

For a moment, it looks like they are about to escape!

Tweedledim and Tweedledank waste that moment by pausing to virtue-signal and congratulate themselves on freeing the spacehorses, and to say that freeing the animals is the only real victory in their whole rebellion. It was all worth it.

It is the single most smug yet stupid line anywhere in the entire canon of science fiction films. No, I am not going to look it up and repeat it word for word, lest you learn the exact words, and the nerve cells in your brain respond to the unseen stupidity rays radiating from the line, and a woeful fate befall you and your heirs.

Dank and Dim then don PETA shirts, and eat vegetarian meals, firebomb pet stores, outlaw circus animals, use green energy, stop all global warming, and virtue signal as hard as they can possibly signal.

Meanwhile, the spacehorses, being dumb animals with no interest in abstract ideas like political freedom, return to their stalls for their evening oats and water, just as they are comfortably habituated to do, except for one brave stallion named Spirit, who races out bold and free into the wastelands! Run, Spirit, run!

But, being raised as a prize domestic pet and hence unable to care for himself in the wild, Spirit immediately falls into a sandpit and is eaten by the Sarlacc.

Of course, the Tweedle twins fail to escape, because everyone fails at everything in this film, and a traffic cop aircraft has them trapped against the cliffside. In a film about liberty and tyranny fighting over the freedom of the galaxy, we spend an hour on a plotline that ends with two doofus clumbzoids being chased down by the meter maids.

Then BB-8 pays their parking ticket, and they go free. No, wait, that does not happen.

Instead, stupid happens. DJ unexpectedly swoops in flying a stolen space yacht, the *SS Deus Ex Machina*, and rescues their worthless hides from the traffic cops.

Please note that DJ had no means of locating the Tweedles and no reason to be in that area.

Please note that, in yet another one-and-done non-fight scene, his ship simply knocks the police ships aside, and they fall down, unhurt but also somehow unable to pursue, and his ship is unharmed. How plot-convenient!

Please note an utter lack of motive for the rescue. The master codebreaker was neither hired by Dim and Dank, nor expressed any interest in being hired. No money changed hands. He has no interest in the Rebellion or their political aspirations, and expresses no pity for them. DJ has no reason to trust, like, or be grateful to the two boneheaded fumbleclowns.

DJ then tells them that this yacht belonged to an arms manufacturer who sold weapons not only to the Empire, but also to the Rebels. Dim and Dank look properly confused. Dank wonders how she can virtue-signal her empty pretense of virtue in a universe where good and evil cannot simply be assigned by identity politics? What happens to class warfare if there are virtuous men among the rich?

DJ cynically tells them that the Empire and the Rebels, Team Tyranny and Team Liberty, are morally equivalent: one should live for oneself. Never join a team! He says this while joining their team, or pretending to. No alarm bells go off in the pointy heads of anyone involved.

Now, the one and only scene where Finn does something heroic and selfless happens after this point.

In a competent movie from the positive matter universe of good, where we live, the first event would be tied to the second: Finn would reject the cynical selfishness of DJ, live up to the sacrificial fortitude demanded of heroes, and fight the impossible odds, tilting at windmills and felling giants with a slingstone; whereupon DJ, impressed, would return like Han Solo during the fatal trench-run over the Death Star and redeem his own selfish ways by becoming a hero as well.

But in a skank movie from the antimatter universe of evil, where this film was made, we see that the moral of the story, as well as the rules of storytelling, are warped, diseased, irrational, and unsightly. In the antimatter universe, nothing connects the one event to the next. Like every other scene in the film, this scene could have been taken out, changed, or even reversed, without any other changes to the film.

Then more stupid happens.

9

NON-PLOT C: GENERAL GENDER STUDIES AND PRINCESS POPPINS

It occurs to me that there is a non-sideplot non-C, a third but painfully boring and trivial series of meaningless yet stupid events happening for no reason. Non-C is set to one side from the main non-plots of non-A and non-B.

On the other hand, as far as I can tell, what I am calling a side-plot might have been meant to be the main action, and what I call the main action might have been a side-plot. Since nothing is coherent, and all is pointless and disconnected, how can one tell minor action from major?

Did I say "action"? As if.

When we last left the ugly, stupid, boring, and unimportant characters no one cares about, the Resistance flotilla was being chased by the Space Nazi clowncar fleet through space.

Emo Vader climbs into his space fighter and makes an attack run on the space cruiser where his Mom, General Ruin, is standing on the bridge. Since he killed his Dad in the last film, maybe he is hoping to make himself an orphan in this. Because Dark Side, or something. Did I mention that he has no motivation for anything he does?

His targeting system locks on his Mom. The letters on his death-screen flash in bright read: MOM SIGHTED! MOM IN RANGE! The radar specially designed to show him where his Mom is standing blinks at him!

His twitching, black-clad, evil finger of his nefarious black right-hand glove inches toward the Death Button, which will open the bomb bay doors and release the Mom-killing missiles!!!

So, then, for no clear reason springing out of any prior event, pity overcomes him, and he aborts the shot. Aha! Another false buildup of tension for no reason, leading to nothing! What clever writing!

Oh, but then the faceless Imperial pilot XP101 in fighter-rocket CUL8R pops ups over the shoulder of Emo Vader, and casually blasts the bridge area with a volley of perfectly ordinary high-explosive space missiles, killing the entire bridge crew instantly, blasting and incinerating them but also peppering their bodies with shrapnel, and then flushing their burnt, lacerated remains out into the merciless vacuum of space, where the effects of explosive decompression kills them a second time long before asphyxiation can kill them a third time.

I have it on good authority that the faceless Imperial pilot XP101 then returns to the flightdeck of the Imperial Doomship *Indomitable*, and goes to the wardroom for a cup of joe and a cigarette, grumbling as he fills out his after-action report on fuel and ordinance expended. He is utterly unaware of who he just shot, since he is a professional serviceman, who handles his missions for the Empire in a professional way. He is the only character in the entire film who ever accomplishes something he sets out to do. He is now my favorite character.

His backstory? After a stormy romance, Expy Wunowan

was married to his childhood sweetheart, the raven-haired Nastra, and the couple now lives in a snug suburban asteroid in the Venom Nebula, with their four children: Sinistro, Invidia, Mon-star, and Zorak, who will be entering the Sith Academy next year, to become an evil space wizard. Congrats to Darth Zorak!

But wait! There is more! The film-perp will not allow faceless Imperial pilot XP101 to get away with accomplishing something in *this* film, where nothing comes to anything and nothing matters!

In the single most absurd abuse of Deus ex Machina machinery since the time the dead Bobby Ewing of *Dallas* popped back to life in the shower with no explanation, General Ruin wakes up from being dead in space, is not burnt nor wounded by shrapnel, is unaffected by explosive decompression, and floats like Mary Poppins back through the torpedo-holes in the hull into the wreckage of the bridge.

She suddenly has Friendly Space Witch powers for no reason and with no explanation.

True, her brother is a Space Wizard. But she has not been trained to use these powers and had never used them before, never expressed the least desire to learn them, nor does she use them after. Floating unharmed through hard vacuum is not, in fact, one of the Force powers any space wizard commands or has ever commanded.

True, her brother in the original trilogy did say she would learn and one day master the Force. Think of how cool this film would have been if she had! Picture her dressed in Jedi robes and carrying a light saber, able to sense the Sith Lord's wicked thoughts from a distance, and hide her future plans from his clairvoyant malice.

But, no, there is no hint that she ever learned anything:

her powers appear only long enough to undo the point of the prior scene. Then they disappear again.

I have it one good authority that she spits on the corpse of fan favorite Admiral Ackbar as she floats back in, since the film-perp wanted to kill him off in order to annoy and disappoint fans, and turn his job over to Girl-General Gender Studies.

To emphasize the magnitude and absurdity of this change, let us change her name again, from General Ruin, to Space Witch.

Shocked crewmen see Space Witch through a glass panel of the bridge door as she stands in hard vacuum. They are in a heated, oxy-nitrogen atmosphere pressurized at fifteen pounds per square inch. They yank open the door.

Let us pause to ponder that.

The average human has about 21 square feet of surface area on his body, which is a little over three thousand square inches. So roughly forty-five thousand pounds of air act on anyone in one atmosphere of pressure opening a door into vacuum.

By way of comparison, according to the current traffic laws of the Commonwealth of Virginia, the maximum gross weight allowed to be carried on a two-axle vehicle is forty thousand pounds, some five thousand pounds less than this. In other words, this amount of weight is too great for any vehicle smaller than a three-axle heavy truck to carry.

That is the amount of weight you would have to stand up against, if you were opening a door like this, in order not to be swept out into space like a leaf in a gale, or, actually, like a ball in a cannon when the powder ignites. It is not called "gentle, gradual decompression," you know.

But this film does not know or care how outer space works.

I am surprised that General Ruin, when she was in zero gee in outer space, did not fall in the direction we call "space-down," travelling in the same direction as the bombs dropped from bomber ships in reel one. We all know objects in outer space are pulled by gravity from the top of the screen to the bottom.

Ruin just opens the door and walks in. Then they rush her to the medical bay, and she goes into a coma, much like most of the audience.

Normally, a character dying and coming back to life is dramatic and impressive. This was not: and that for two reasons.

First, it comes out of nowhere for no reason, and hence has no heft, no emotional weight. It is meaningless.

Second, nothing comes of it, not even the fact that Space Witch is now alive. No one expresses surprise or bafflement or awe that she can spacewalk without a suit and return herself from the dead after being blown through a space-ship hull. If she had died and stayed dead, maybe two other scenes would have needed a reshoot. This character does not really do anything else aside from (1) shooting Hotshot on the bridge to end his dipstick mutiny and (2) bidding Mopey farewell on the Salt Planet.

Space Witch is whisked offscreen to the medical bay, where, for some odd reason, we are treated to no scenes whatever of her bumping her head or slipping on medical fluid. Such comedy antics of the Emergency Room are reserved for black space-males.

Then more stupid happens.

Hotshot Pilot, now demoted to Dogcatcher, goes to the new commanding officer, who is not fan favorite Admiral Ackbar, but instead is a thin-faced crone in a sadly sagging evening dress with brightly-dyed purple hair, hereafter called Girl-General Gender Studies van Grievance.

He politely asks her what plan he and his men should be following to preserve their besieged and dying flotilla from the hot pursuit at that moment shooting at them. She replies by telling him men are the inferior sex, and are not allowed to hear plans invented by Gender Studies crones with purple hair.

He must obey orders without question, mechanically and mindlessly. After all, that is the principle and the philosophy the rebellion has stood for during the entire Star Wars canon of films, novels, and comics: The Empire stands for freedom and initiative, and the Rebels are fighting to bring about a regime based on perfect mindless obedience of authority. How clear. How reasonable.

This conversation takes place in public, in earshot of Hotshot Dogcatcher's men, who, for some reason, are all women. Just to make sure that the whole process is carried out with proper military courtesy and decorum, the commanding officer in the sagging evening dress smacks Hotshot in the face with a lemon meringue pie and squirts an entire bottle of seltzer water down his pants.

The scene leaves me pondering questions: What is the point of this scene? What is the film-perp trying to accomplish?

What is the motive of General Grievance? Why such fierce odium?

Maybe she was the other sister of the oriental bombardier killed in the first reel, and so hates and loathes Hotshot with an irrational fervor.

Or maybe in her misspent youth, her virginal love for some or other devilishly handsome yet reckless rogue led to heartbreak, a pregnancy, and a hushed-up scandal, forcing her into military service to hide her shame: and her burning hatred of all young roguish men festered and grew as years passed.

Or maybe the film-perp thinks all creepy old women hate and loathe handsome young soldiers who routinely risk life and limb to save their worthless, withered, dry, infertile, post-menopausal lives.

Or whatever. From what we see on the screen, the emotion comes out of nowhere and has no point.

Then more stupid happens. Four more capital ships and countless escort craft of the escape flotilla are then blasted to bits by the Empire, and lost with all hands while Gender Studies continues to have no plan and to do nothing.

Then came the only scene in this whole circus-train-wreck of a movie that actually made sense to me and had a point: Hotshot leads a mutiny, and relieves Girl-General Gender Studies of command, and tosses her into the brig while the grateful survivors, who otherwise would have been killed to death by the immeasurable incompetence of the aging female leadership, cheer, throw confetti, and pop the bubbly corks.

Girl-General Gender Studies is thrust in front of a firing squad gathered on the hangar deck and summarily executed by laser-rifle. Dogcatcher announces that he, unlike her, has a plan to save them: he explains to the suddenly silent and big-eyed soldiers that he sent the chubby Wrench Monkey with the cattleprod and the cowardly Token Stormtrooper, Tweedledank and Twee-dledim, to planet Swank to hire a Codebreaker because a random dwarfy orange bartender over the holo-phone told him to, and Dim and Dank will disguise themselves as left-handed ice cream spatula salesmen, then sneak aboard the superdeathship crewed by stormtroopers, killer-robots, and evil space wizards, and discombobulate the McGuffin for six minutes. That is the plan! With a flourish, Dogcatcher holds up his hands to welcome their cheers of gratitude for his greatness and cunning.

Without missing a beat, the laser-rife firing squad sharply executes an about face, and shoots the Dogcatcher to death immediately. The Resistance then hires a six-year-old kindergarten-dropout named Booger to lead them, and he does a better job than anyone heretofore.

No, I am sorry, that part was not actually in the movie. It was an hallucination caused by a brain aneurysm resulting from repeated sharp blows of the railgun-launched stupidity hammer shooting out of the screen and through my aching skull.

In fact, what happens is that Ruin the Friendly Space Witch, rising from her sick bed, totters weakly on trembling legs up to the Dogcatcher, bold leader of the bold mutiny, and, while he is staring cross-eyed at her awesomeness, she slowly raises the gun she had hidden behind her back and slowly shoots him. This is but a stun-charge, however, so he is flipped in a comedy-relief pratfall across the deck.

Of course, Hotshot lowers his gun when he sees it is Space Witch back from the dead. Maybe he remembers how cool she was in the original trilogy. At that point, all she had to do was talk to him, maybe even tell him the plan. Which she does later. But, no. This idiot movie has to make sure that no heroism, no chivalry, no courtesy is shown to be anything but idiotic. Hotshot's respect for his princess is answered by her zoinking him.

For those of you keeping track, this is the third time an overaged or undersized girl has bested a stalwart, well-muscled, and battle-hardened veteran in a one-and-done shoot out. Suddenly the error of having legions of

Stormtroopers shoot at rebels is clear: if only ninety-pound cleaning ladies, stewardesses, co-eds, and cheerleaders had been armed and sent against the rebels, led by seventy-pound hags, crones, and termagants, the Empire would have cleaned their clock!

Hotshot is held to court-martial, convicted of having testosterone while being male, and shot by a firing squad of ninety-pound cleaning ladies, stewardesses, co-eds, and cheerleaders.

No, wait, that does not happen. Instead, he is given a weapon and returned to duty. Because the film-perp forgot that he was the ringleader of a mutiny.

Then, more stupid happens.

Girl-General Gender Studies van Grievance is back in charge again, even though Space Witch is up and about, and reveals her grand plan: the four hundred remaining rebels will sneak away in spaceboats to their base on the Salt Planet, leaving the Imperial Deathfleet to chase an empty cruiser across the galaxy.

For no reason whatsoever, this lame-brained, dumb-ucket plan was kept secret from everyone in the rebellion, include the crewmen who had prepped the spaceboats for launch and programmed the route of escape to the Salt Planet into the navigation computers.

Let me emphasize the fact that dumb plot points count for double dumb if and when they could have been corrected or explained by adding a single scene, or even a single line, to the film. In this case, one line stating that, since it was thought to be an impossible technology to track a fleeing fleet through hyperspace, the rebel High Command believes there is a traitor aboard, someone somehow passing ship location information to the enemy. Without knowledge of who or where this traitor is, no part of the secret escape plan can be revealed. It is on a strictly need-to-know basis.

See how simple that is? Instead of a scene where General Gender Studies mocks and belittles her best fighter-pilot for the sin of being brave and bold and manly in an ever-loving space-adventure flick, the matter could have been handled with ordinary military courtesy.

Hotshot could have expressed bewilderment or discontent. "How can we not trust the men who have fought and died side by side these many years?" and she could have answered, "The Space Princess made this plan. She has gotten us out of many a tight scrape before!" And then he could have remembered how wise and good the rebel leader was, and his eyes would light up with hope and faith.

That could have been a good scene. Instead we have lazy, sleazy dreck.

The rebels are loaded aboard unshielded, slow, and weaponless spaceboats which cannot run nor fight.

When I saw this scene, I thought the spaceboats had been rigged with cloaking devices, or stealth gear, or somehow had been made radar-invisible: but no. When the super-duper secret plan of Purple Haired Hag is revealed, all that is said is "the First Order is scanning for big ships. They are not monitoring for little transports!"

Except that they are, and start blasting them out of space one by one.

Remember how Hotshot Pilot got demoted to Dogcatcher because the butterfingered crew of the bomber fleets all died on his watch? Well, the entire rebellion is decimated, cut down from four hundred people to forty in one barrage, thanks to the idiotic Girl-General Gender Studies.

Then, more stupid happens. Space Witch comes to Gender Studies, and they say a heartfelt, tearful farewell to each other, as if these two characters were supposed to know each other. Since they had not had any scenes together before this, or so much as waved hello, I am not sure why the film-perp expects us suddenly to get teary-eyed over the end of an alleged close friendship which has never been seen ere now.

Space Witch tells Gender Studies that it is time for her, and for her wig, to commit a seppuku via kamikaze in atonement for her idiotic generalship, the death of nine-tenths of the men in her command, her smug attitude, and her bad hair. Gender Studies will ram her spaceship into the pursuing fleet at lightspeed.

Gender Studies objects that a robot could pilot the ship during this suicide run, or maybe a mutineer who otherwise would be condemned to the firing squad. She points out that this form of attack could not possibly work under the rules established in nine movies and countless books and comics: ships in hyperspace pass through a conduit or tube outside of normal spacetime, unable to affect nor to be affected by objects in real space. If such a ship maneuver could possibly work, it would have been a staple part of fleet combat for all of Galactic history.

Space Witch tells Gender Studies that suicide is required by her noble pagan ancestors, and that to destroy oneself, thus obliterating the image of God in man, pleases the devils all witches secretly worship. All hail the Great God Tao of Mongo!

Burly and chortling marine roughnecks, Hotshot the Pilot, a group of incels from MGTOW, and a bevy of pretty stewardesses, co-eds and cheerleaders who actually like being girls, all gather to stuff the screaming and struggling ex-general hag into a bag, and chain her to the pilot's chair, and put a brick on the accelerator petal. Smirking, the Space

Witch and the MGTOW toss ironic farewells to the doomed hagbag from behind the docking portholes as the engines roar into a high-pitched overload...

Or, no, wait, that did not happen. That would have made sense. Instead, the purple-haired hag blows herself and half the enemy fleet into vapor in a spectacular flourish of special effects.

The scene is visually dramatic, and as well done as anything ever seen in a sci-fi spectacle. It looked good.

It was dumb as a box of space-rocks, but it looked good.

10

NON-CLIMAX 1: NON-FIGHT ON THE FLAGSHIP

Meanwhile, in the throneroom, Snoopy is done torturing Mary Sue, and so he Force-chokes her to death, and telekinetically rips her head off, and her skull is cleaned and set in his smoking parlor as an ashtray.

No, wait, what actually happens is Snoopy orders Emo Vader to kill Mary Sue, even though Snoopy just got done saying he knew darn well Emo was emotionally unstable. I think the film-perpetrator thought there was some sort of romantic chemistry or hint of mutual attraction between the wooden-faced, unsightly, short-haired, and unfeminine boyish girl, and the pasty-faced, long-haired, hysterical girlish boy, but, if so, yeech, and, if so, no smallest hint of such a thing ever came on screen.

I have seen the actress in other photos all dolled up, and she is perfectly attractive, even glamorous. I am sure the actor likewise is handsome in his off time. But in this film, the characters are portrayed in such an unflattering light, ill-garbed, graceless and ungainly, that the idea of either one of them engaging in romantic union with another living organism is a crime against Darwin.

In any case, if Emo was allegedly sweet on Mary Sue, it is stupid for Snoopy to assign him as her executioner. (He is demanding a show of loyalty from the kid who killed his own father the last episode?)

To no one's surprise, Emo strikes down Snoopy, not Mary, even while Snoopy is boasting that he can read Emo's mind, and sees his intent to smite his enemy.

Except that, if he were reading his mind, why was Snoopy fooled? Is there yet another unexplained new Force Power that allows Emo to hide his thoughts even while they are being read? Again, this is something a single line of dialog could have cleared up.

So the absurdly powerful Sith lord failed to sense what is happened around him, and he is cut in half. There is no epic boss battle here. One more one-and-done fight scene. He gets no dying words, no ominous last curse, nothing.

Then Emo and Mary team up for no reason and fight the Praetorian guard in red. I should not complain, because it actually is a fight scene where people fight, not a one-and-done.

But I will complain. The poor, awkward actress playing Mary Sue swings her lightsaber around like a farmwife with a broom trying to shoo away crows, and the stunt men have to swing and miss in order not to brain the actress when she misses her mark.

Why the lightsabers are not merely chopping right through the weapons of the baddies is not clear, nor why the two Jedi with a handwave do not merely knock one and all spinning like ninepins.

In any case, there are no thrills and no tension, and, of course, the girl saves the guy two or three times from certain death, but she needs no help from him.

She has one slick maneuver where she locks blades in a

corps-a-corps, retracts the lightsaber blade, letting it drop, catching it with her off hand, and ignites it again through the foe's body, in an elaborate counterparry-riposte. In all the fight scenes of this whole long purgatory of a film, that is the only time anyone does anything that actually looked interesting.

In short order, Emo and Mary chop and stir-fry the mooks into mincemeat, but then both implore the other to join their side. But the writer never invented a philosophy motivating Empire nor rebels, nor invented personalities or motives for either character, so neither had anything to say.

Instead they start wrestling over the remaining lightsaber with their brains. If they had brains.

Then more stupid happens.

Meanwhile, the sneak team of Tweedles snuck aboard the flagship because the Master Codebreaker had picked the lock on the force-screen surrounding the ship. (And, yes, picking a lock on a force-screen is just as dumb an idea as it sounds, but it made the character look competent.)

Annoying Bot Billiard Ball disguises himself by throwing a trashcan upside down over his chassis, and an evil Nazi Eightball spots him and rats him out by beeping and blinking. So they are caught immediately.

Evil Nazi Eightball. Let the syllables of that idea rattle in your brain like dice in a dice cup for just a moment. If you had any doubts about whether the film-perp is trolling the audience, and flipping us the bird for being so stupid as to enjoy space opera, let those doubts rest.

The prisoners are taken, not to the brig, but to the hanger deck where all the fightercraft and walking tanks, with high-explosive ordinance loaded and engines fully fueled, are docked.

We are treated to the scene of Dim and Dank being

thrown on the metal deck with stormtroopers in jackboots trampling their faces, a sensation each audience member also vividly knows.

The dipstick twins are lying there with death-guns shoved up their nostrils so that their walnut-sized brains can be vaporized and their empty skulls exploded. I admit I did sort of like this scene, because their plan was so stupid they deserved to be caught, and because pain was inflicted on them.

Then DJ "Don't Join" Codebreaker comes sauntering by with a shrug and a farewell, saying he had cut a deal with the Empire and betrayed them.

I admit was the only plot twist in this whole intestine-twisted garbage film that made sense, since it was properly set up. DJ clearly had never had any reason to save nor serve the Tweedle twins, but the prospect of luring them from planet Swank and straight into the hands of the Empire and collecting a bounty would give him a legitimate, that is, understandable, motivation for his character as established. Well done! After all, this was not the man the bartender said could be trusted: he was a random crook the Tweedles found in jail who sized them up and played them for chumps.

I should say it almost made sense: but not quite. When did he cut this deal? By radio, before they snuck aboard, or after they were caught? He has nothing to offer the Empire once caught, so it had to have been before boarding: But in that case, what was all that idiotic business with the Evil Nazi Eightball?

Or perhaps he did offer them something: at this point, Master Codebreaker says he knows the super-duper super-secret plan of Girl-General Gender Studies, and that the spaceboats are disguised by some sort of cloaking device, but he knows the secret frequency whereof, which he told the Empire.

This, unfortunately, fills a plot hole by opening a plot canyon: there is no scene where the spaceboats are said to be rigged out with sci-fi cloaking devices. It is, however, established in a previous film that cloaking devices do exist in the Star Wars universe, but cannot be rigged onto small ships.

I am not sure when Dim and Dank are told the super-secret plan, or who told them, but I was listening to the film in Spanish at this point, so let's just assume some idiot idiotically told them over the un-shielded and un-encrypted space-radio, and Dim and Dank, master spies of super intrigue, shouted and heliographed and semaphored the information to each other across the cabin while DJ was casually standing nearby smoking a death stick. Whatever. Who cares?

So, the twin Tweedles are about to be lasered to death, and the average IQ of the galaxy raised by a small but definite fraction, when Deus ex Machina machinery grinds into motion.

Remember the purple-haired hag who committed suicide and sent her soul straight to hell when she rammed her ship through the Imperial flagship at lightspeed?

Remember that, in additional to the stealthy sneak team of the Tweedles, bot, and Codebreaker, Mary Sue and Emo Vader are also aboard the flagship, wrestling over a lightsaber. I am happy to report that they are all killed instantly, incinerated, and vaporized during the lightspeed collision.

Or, no, wait, that did not happen. That would have made sense.

The flagship is cracked in two by the attack. Emo Vader

and Mary Sue, bodies Swiss-cheesed by shrapnel, are blown out into space, and die from the explosive decompression, but then resuscitate, and fly back to the ship across empty space like Superboy and Supergirl, while Daisy Ridley sings Louis Lane's themesong *'Can You Read My Mind?'* from *Superman the Motion Picture.*

Actually, that did not happen either, but would be in keeping with the prior scenes.

What really happened is this. Mary Sue and Emo Vader are wrestling over Luke's lightsaber, because (so I assume) they are trying to kill each other. The lightsaber snaps in half, and, for no reason, explodes. Both are flung onto their buttocks, and knocked witless. Well, more witless.

Like well-nigh every other fight scene in this flick, in the struggle between Emo and Mary, there is no cleverness, no maneuvers, no tactics, no struggle, no effort, no heroism, no nothing.

Then, a while later, Admiral Hux walks in, steps blithely over the corpse of Supreme Leader Snoopy, and glances down at the unconscious body of Emo Vader. Wisely, he draws his sidearm, no doubt thinking of putting a plasma bolt through the boy's head and saving the Empire from the most incompetent Sith lord imaginable. I was cheering for Hux. He is now my favorite character.

Ah, but in this movie, no one actually accomplishes anything he starts to do, no matter who he is, and no matter what the action is, large or small.

So, Emo wakes up, Force-chokes Hux a bit to rattle his teeth, and Hux hails him as the new Emperor. When and how Mary Sue woke up and escaped the wreckage of the flagship is not mentioned. Maybe she just flew across empty space like supergirl.

Meanwhile, back in the flight hangar, Tweedledank the

Zoink-dwarf is dragging a semi-comatose Tweedledim along the deck. This is the second time the undersized dwarf woman is seen dragging the black spaceman by the foot, so I assume the film writer has some sort of weird fetish about this.

Then a character named Phasmid or something like that, a splendid-looking she-stormtrooper in chrome armor, comes marching out of the mist and smoke of the ruined deck, with her squad of killers goose-stepping behind her. It looked good. I wish I could see the movie, a sequel to Star Wars, that this scene should have come from.

In that good version of this movie, Phasmid would have been the Darth Vader figure to Finn, what Granny Goodness of Apokalips was to Scott Free in Jack Kirby's Fourth World. Phasmid, after all, was Finn's CO, the leader he once admired and served. In a properly paced and written story arc leading to a satisfactory conclusion, Finn would have escaped from Phasmid in the first movie, fought and lost horribly in the second, but after driving himself in merciless training to hone his fighting skills, stepped forth a final time, to face this nemesis, and, after a tough, drawn-out fight, not without some cunning moves on his part, defeated Phasmid, winning the girl, and saving the day.

Oh, and there should have been a girl to save. I suggest Vietnamese actress Veronica Ngo, who played Tien the evil elf in the Netflix film BRIGHT. She is a total hottie, and would have made a perfect love interest for Finn. Would that an actress as pretty as she had been in this movie!

And Phasmid would have been a boy, because the idea of girl stormtroopers is silly.

Instead what happens is the troopers blast the escaping rebels, and the two rebels both die instantly. No, wait, the two rebels take cover, and, uh, pick up weapons troopers dropped during the ship-ramming, and return fire. But they are outnumbered! It actually looks like something exciting is about to happen!

Nope. A walking tank, conveniently loaded with ammo and conveniently right at hand, now opens fire on the troopers and scatters them. It would have been satisfying had this tank been piloted by DJ the Codebreaker, with the plot twist that he was impressed with the heroism of the rebels, stung by guilt, and was willing to risk his life in atonement.

Nope. The top of the convertible tank falls off for no reason, and we see that Annoy-bot Billiard Ball is piloting the tank. The audience erupts in groans of disbelief and four-letter Anglo-Saxon words expressing contempt and incredulity. Why isn't the tank shooting gold coins at the stormtroopers? Who builds tanks as convertibles?

Please note that at this point the annoying robo-ball has defeated in personal combat or gunfights more enemy soldiers than every other character in this film combined.

More to the point, since this robot was with the sneaky sneak team when they were captured, and, indeed, it was the Billiard Ball who gave them away when the Evil Nazi Eightball who penetrated their disguises, how in the world was the annoy-droid supposed to end up on the flight deck behind the controls of a walking tank as opposed to being shoved immediately into a robot disintegration box? Well, maybe he rolled away in the confusion or something. Whatever. Nothing matters.

Phasmid curbstomps Tweedledim in one more grotesque example of Chrome-on-Black racist violence. Of course, she is a girl, so she can beat Dim like a rented mule while he howls like a whipped hound-dog.

But then Tweedledank, dwarf girl soldier girl, opens fire

on Phasmid to save her brother in arms! There is a cool moment when Dank's blaster fire simply bounces off Phasmid's armor, which I liked, since one wonders why stormtroopers in Star Wars wear armor otherwise.

Phasmid returns fire and Dank hides, which I also liked, since, for a moment, it looked as if something real, involving real danger, was about to happen.

Nope. Phasmid punches Dim off a ledge and she confidently turns her back. But then in the most obvious and predictable trope ever, an elevator platform rises into view with Dim, safe and sound, standing there with a space baseball bat in his hand.

How plot-convenient that an unexpected space elevator just so happened so unexpectedly to be in just the position like a catcher's mitt for no reason unexpectedly to catch our incompetent hero in mid-plummet!

When Phasmid turns, he coldcocks the girl in the face with a cowardly blow, knocking her into a flaming pit in yet another unsatisfying and cowardly, undignified, and unchivalrous ending to what might have been a good fight scene.

The film-perp wanted there to be some memorable banter or witty quip exchanged between the two, but he could not think of anything, so they just both drop jaws open and stupid comes out.

"You were always scum!" she hisses as she dies the death.

"*Rebel* scum!" he grins, looking proud. Because, uh, this means... wait. I don't get it.

Dim and Dank depart from the broken-in-half flagship with no further ado and make it to the Salt Planet, which they had no way of knowing where it was, or where on the whole globe, which mountain range in what hemisphere, the hidden rebel base might have been hidden.

Meanwhile none of the Imperial crewmen depart the broken-in-half flagship, nor does any of the unwrecked ships in the Imperial fleet notice or open fire the fleeing rebels. Perhaps there was confusion while the Empire ships raced to rescue their survivors, but this was not onscreen, so it is just another unexplained lapse in the script.

Dim and Dank now race to the secret hideout mountain on Planet Salt. Their stolen Imperial spaceboat makes it into the invincible super gate of the escape proof hideout just before the super gate slams shut, but only their ship and no other makes it inside. Somehow. Then the crack rebel marksmen pepper the flimsy spaceboat with blaster fire, but each and every single bolt misses the Tweedle twins. Somehow. Nothing matters.

Of course, since the Tweedle twins are responsible for the decimation and death and destruction of the rebels fleeing on the transports, since they failed to practice normal info security and let DJ Codebreaker pass the idiot escape plan to the Empire, I was hoping that after a fond welcome, the Billiard Ball would play back its robo tapes, all their dialog be heard, their crimes be discovered and Dim and Dank be burned alive by firing squad nonetheless.

But that would have made sense. Nothing in this waste-basket-of-vomit-in-the-washing-machine of a film makes sense.

11

NON-CLIMAX 2: NON-FIGHT AT THE
ESCAPE-PROOF HIDEOUT

Tweedledim, Tweedledank, Hotshot Mutineer, and Space Witch are now hidden under an armored mountain on a salt-covered planet. The rebel lair has one massively giant iron door leading in and out, and, unlike a warren dug by something as wise as a groundhog or bunny-rabbit, there is no other escape exit, no bolt hole.

The rebels lock themselves in with no way out. Because they are morons.

They radio for help to their allies on the Outer Rim, and get the answering machine. Their Outer Rim allies stand them up and will not return any phone calls. Can't say I blame them.

Space Witch then gives a speech. Who cares?

The Empire lands in force, which consists of half a dozen walking tanks and one aircraft. Hardly D-Day. Not even Dunkirk. More like the magnitude of the battle scene in Disney's *Bedknobs and Broomsticks* where one witch and a war museum full of English ghosts repel a single U-Boat of Nazi invaders from landing at the little village of Pepperinge Eye.

Which, now that I think about it, has a number of parallels with this scene: a witch and a group of children armed with antiques and special effects fend off Nazis by means of a trick involving empty suits of armor, which, like a force-holo of a Jedi master, can seem to be stabbed and shot, but really cannot suffer harm.

This might have been an exciting fight scene if there had been any fight. As it was, the rebels were so obviously and absurdly overmatched that there was no tension. I am not saying all fights have to be even-steven to be exciting, but if the outcome is sure, the story has to take another angle. The film-perpetrator could have followed the example of Disney's *Davy Crockett*, portraying the brave resignation of the doomed soldiers during their last stand at the Alamo; but he did not.

In a visually splendid scene, the rebels race across the sand on broken and antique speeders. The Empire brings up a laser siege gun described as being based on miniature Death Star technology and prepares to use it against the massively giant iron door. The speeders rush in, guns blazing.

The crossfire from the Imperial walkers and air cover is too great. Hotshot pilot, apparently having learned his lesson not to spend lives needlessly in battle, calls a retreat. All the speeders peel off to the left and right.

All but one.

One lone speeder is piloted by a fighting man who will not flinch and will not turn aside. It is Finn! Finn, the defector, who has spent all his efforts erenow trying to escape and run away. Now he is a man. Now he will not run away.

He points this doomed craft straight at the mouth of the titanic super-cannon. He intends to ram it. Voices in alarm over the radio order or beg him to break off the attack.

Impatiently he tosses his headset aside. He face is grim and set. Death is nigh. He hits the throttle, closes his eyes, and prepares to meet his fate.

Dang! I get chills just thinking about it.

I almost fell in love with this film at that moment. I was prepared to forgive all: because, for a moment, for one glorious yet deceptive moment, it looked as if an absurd and abused comic relief character, Tweedledim the slapstick goof, was going to transform before my eyes into Finn, the hard-as-nails ex-Stormtrooper, the one man who, having seen them from within, knew the true depravity of the First Order. He had been one of them. He was willing to make the ultimate sacrifice to thwart their terrible victory.

Of course, I should mention that his commanding officer, Dogcatcher, does say that the speedster, even if crashed into the mouth of the siege cannon, would do no significant damage. That, and the fact that the moron did not trigger his ejector seat at the last moment, hints that perhaps all this build up was simply false: he was not making any sort of noble sacrifice, he was just preparing to kill himself out of despair, or maybe boredom for being trapped in so pointless a film.

What happens instead is so stupid, such bad writing, that my fingers grow weak on the keys.

By bad writing, I do not mean it was merely not to my taste. I do not mean that it was unexpected. Nor do I mean that my hopes as a fan were smashed, as if the film-perpetrator thought himself to have a sacred duty to the gods of subversion to smash my hopes and to make me, and my heroes, feel and look like fools.

Make no mistake, the maker of this film was motivated my malice, the malice of the Pharisees, a sense of lofty superiority which mocks the honest desires of ticket-buying loyal customers as contemptible benighted sentiment, which he says it is his divine mission, as a guru of the higher truth, to shatter and hold up to scorn.

But that is not what makes this scene bad writing. It was technically bad, mechanically bad, objectively bad, not as a matter of opinion, but as a matter of fact.

Judge for yourself:

In the final moment before he drives his speeder into the muzzle of the super-cannon, Tweedledank, the zoink-powered Wrench Monkey, yet again is shown knocking him on his buttocks. She swoops down out of the sun, not to smash into the cannon herself and spare him the need to do so, but to smash into his craft, knocking them both tumbling aside into the ground, out of the way and into irrelevance.

I note in passing that the butterfingered bombers in the first reel were destroyed by ramming, the police craft of planet Swank knocked aside by ramming, and the Imperial flagship, along with a dozen lesser ships of the line, were obliterated by ramming. It seems to be something of a fetish with this director.

Dim crawls from the broken wreckage, miraculously unhurt, and asks the dying dwarf why she did so dumb a thing. She replies that the war will not be won by fighting who we hate, but by saving who we love!

She steals a kiss from him. In the same frame of the movie screen, as she is kissing him, the energy beam from the cannon hits the giant iron doors like a piledriver, breaking them asunder, presumably killing the entire base compliment instantly! Or, if any survived, they are doomed by Dank's action to quick death by firing squad, or, if condemned instead to the spice mines of Kessel, to a slow one. Thanks, Dank.

Or mayhap the other members of the rebellion were not

loved by anyone, certainly by no one in the audience, and did not need to be saved.

Tweedledank singlehandedly just tossed victory into the lap of the space-Nazis. Self-sacrifice is apparently allowed for crusty old purple-haired hags, but not for black space-males. They must be emasculated and robbed of agency.

The reason why I argue that this is objectively bad, mechanically bad, and not just a plot twist that happens not to please me is this: There are three components to any criticism of art. One is to look at the mechanics of the art form, regardless of content. That is an objective matter. The poem either has fourteen rhyming lines or does not; if it is a thirteen line poem, or blank verse, good bad or indifferent, it is not a sonnet. The next component is a judgement call: did the artist achieve the effect he was attempting? Was the audience moved as he was trying to move them? The final is subjective: did I like it? Was I moved? A critic can, for example, be no fan of horror movies, or even dislike the whole genre, and still be able to tell John Carpenter's *Halloween* is well-made and Ed Wood's *Plan Nine From Outer Space* is not.

In this case, in story telling of any kind, in film or print, any plot point needs set up and follow through if it is to be emotionally satisfying. The set up for a character like Rick Blaine in *Casablanca*, or Han Solo in *Star Wars*, who at first wants no part of the fight is to have him show his reluctance. Hence the scene in *Casablanca* where Rick looks on indifferently as Ugarte is arrested and executed; hence the line in *Star Wars* where Han will not stir a foot to rescue the princess until he is reassured that she is rich. That is the set up. The follow-through is the about-face: when Rick sends away the woman he loves, despite the personal cost to him, or when Han returns unexpectedly to swoop out of the sun and blast Vader's pursuit-ship as it is closing in on Luke for the kill.

We saw the set up for Finn's reluctance in this last film and in this one. He attempts to steal an escape pod, and is zoinked by a zoink-dwarf with a zoink-wand. The follow-through was the about-face and the noble sacrifice to save his friends. Except that the suicide run is said over the radio to be in vain: a pointless gesture. Either Finn would have destroyed the gun by ramming it, or not. If not, it is not a real about-face. It is just a wasted character trying to waste himself to escape this wasteland of a film. But if it would have worked, preventing the sacrifice (at the sacrifice of everyone else) prevents any follow-through on the character arc: he is still, through no fault of his own, back where Rick and Han started out.

Good, bad or indifferent is another matter. Whether you personally liked it or not is another matter. On an objective level, having an event that robs all the meaning out of the set up event, and then leads nowhere to nothing, is a mechanical error in story telling. Story telling consists of telling about meaningful events, not meaningless ones. Even if you want to tell a nihilistic story, whose point is that life is pointless, the story itself must be told in a pointed way, and the events in the story must be meaningful in order to carry the message to the audience, even if that message says that meaning is illusion.

Note again the stupid reversal of sexual roles. Just as Mary Sue, woman with no training, repeatedly saved Emo Vader, trained Sith lord, during their pointless fight with the Red Guard, so, too, here is the woman saving the man. Except, in this case, Dank is saving Dim from the heroic masculine impulse of the Spartans at Thermopylae, or the charity of the saints: *Greater love hath no man than this, that a man lay down his life for his friends*. Well, not today. Not on Rian Johnson's watch!

Of course, even had Dim not been stopped, the theme and message here would have been a little puzzling to say the least. Committing suicide as a combat maneuver may be proper for some pagan Emperor-worshiping Japanese Zero-pilot, but not for the commanding admiral of a fleet, nor something done in defiance of direct orders as a futile and meaningless gesture.

This awkward (and, frankly, unsightly) kiss is the first moment I had any idea that there was supposed to be anything romantic between these two. I am not sure where the film-perp thought he had shown any attraction between them. Maybe the scene where they spit three lines of technobabble at each other? So the emotion motivating the act was not properly set up. It came out of nowhere.

The Spartan wife tells her husband to return with his shield or on it, since only deserters and cowards throw the heavy shields away as they break ranks to run in panic, and only the honored dead are carried back atop their shields. Dank by her actions says the opposite: do not sacrifice for the cause. Desert the cause the moment it demands true sacrifice. Your feelings come first.

Oh? You do not think what Dank did counts as a desertion? She took herself and another soldier out of the fight in a deliberate act of self-maiming sabotage. Whether it is technically desertion or no, I leave to the JAG officers to sort out. In her heart, she left the cause, and wrote off the lives of all her comrades, to save her hunk.

And this is the point, where the film preaches desertion, when the film passes the nadir of badness and actually becomes something offensive, and even pernicious: a bad influence, something impressionable children cannot be allowed to see.

We see Tweedledim hauling Dank's corpse (I hope) or unconscious body (I fear) across the salt flats, where there is neither cover nor concealment, so the Imperial snipers kill them instantly. No, sorry, wishful thinking again. They get safely into the base before the mechanized infantry or the supersonic flying machines of the enemy can make it. They are faster afoot. For some reason.

Then the Empire lobs an atom bomb into the broken door, instantly obliterating all personnel in a microsecond. Or, no, instead they, uh, do something else, involving standing the walking tanks in a motionless line, and not moving forward.

Mary Sue, somehow back in the Millennium Falcon, swoops in out of nowhere, and blasts three TIE fighters in one shot. And this is the first time she ever touched a vehicle-mounted ack-ack gun! Being the moderator's girlfriend is really convenient when playing *Edge of the Empire* like this. He does not even make you roll dice, and you can write any skill you want on your character sheet whenever you want it, and have it at expert or master level immediately, no matter what it says on your skill tree.

Some fighters chase her around for a bit, but she flies through a labyrinth of crystal columns, and something happens to them. Who cares? We already saw the same scene, done better, in a prior film when she flew through the interiors of the gigantic wrecks of starships she had been clambering over every workday of her life, so that she legitimately knew every nook and sharp turn. Here, Chewie is at the controls, and it's a cave no one has ever seen before, so it makes less sense.

Nor was there any tension. Unlike farmboy Luke's

dangerous trench-run down the Death Star, where he is the second or third pilot to attempt it, and where he has just seen the previous pilot blown to bits before his eyes, there is no sense of tension here. We know Mary Sue is unkillable. Even if her ship blows up, she can just Mary Poppins across space, then fly without a space suit into and through the enemy flagship at lightspeed.

Then, more stupid happens. Master Mopey shows up inside the escape-proof hideout, and coldly bids his sister farewell. She tells him to go out and kill her son that he may die the death.

Since this is the first time, as best I recall, she so much as mentions the boy, whatever emotion should have been present, sorrow, regret, guilt, or stern resolve, is not present. Instead, the old lady sounds as tired as the audience feels.

She says the Ben Solo she raised as a child is gone: he is evil, and evil is all-powerful and hope is always futile in this universe. Mopey, for a single moment, remembers he is Luke, and says that no one is ever truly gone.

This is, of course, the opposite of everything he said before this point. But the film-perp cares nothing about consistency of tone, theme, character.

In any other movie, this might be foreshadowing a redemption or about-face for Emo, but not here. Don't be silly.

Mopey departs without a word of farewell to C3PO or R2D2, allegedly his lifelong friends. Yes, they were in this film. No, they did not do anything, and did not affect the action. Chewbacca was in the film also, but he did nothing except knock down a door and eat a penguin-bunny. Another wasted asset. Another lost opportunity.

Out on the salt flats, Master Mopey and his nephew Emo face each other. Who cares? I want them both to die.

Emo vaunts, but Mopey says there is one last Jedi left. Wonder who that is? My money is on the slave stableboy from pointless scene 16.

Emo slashes Mopey in half, but then realizes Mopey is not making any footprints in the salt. Mopey is some sort of astral whatchamacallit.

This is a power no Jedi previously had, but which the Force of Plot Contrivance contrives to thrust onstage.

The scene makes no sense, since Mopey quite clearly announced his intention to kill Emo, and got a blessing from Emo's mother to commit the killing. But he is only an illusion, so he could not hurt a fly, because he is not physically present. So, what was the point?

He is clearly not trying to delay or stall the assault, because there is no reason he could know or guess which would make him think a delay would help anyone. As best he knows, the rebels are trapped in the escape-proof hideout, and, thanks to Dank, the gates are shattered.

Then Mopey vanishes, and we see him back on planet Mopey, where he vanishes a second time, and instantly dies of nothing for no reason.

I said no farewell to this absurd mockery to my beloved childhood hero merely because the event was portrayed in an emotionally dead and neutral way. If he had choked on a fishbone and fallen headfirst into bowl of green milk and drowned with only his nose and mouth submerged, the death scene could not have been duller or stupider.

Then Yoda appears on the battlefield, blasts Emo to death with lightningbolts, and electrocutes the tank crews, who waste their last ammo and their dying moments shooting futile blaster bolts through the madly giggling holograph of a goblin puppet!

Except that does not happen, even though Yoda, who

can now throw lightning from beyond the grave, should win every battle forever after this way. But who wants to win battles? No, Luke delays the assault for no particular reason and dies for no particular reason.

Meanwhile, in a rare moment of logic, Hotshot pilot deduces that if Mopey entered the escape-proof base, there must be an open escape exit somewhere. It is a false deduction, because Mopey is a projection, and never actually entered the base.

But then they find an opening anyway! For no reason!

And it is blocked! For no reason!

But it is only blocked by big rocks, and they are military men sitting on a pile of highly explosive ordinance, energy weapons, and aviation fuel, and so they could blast through the blockage in short order.

Or they could ask Leia Poppins to float down to this part of the base and wave her hand and have happy children, while singing *Just a Spoonful of Sugar*, lift and float the rocks away while cheerful cartoon penguins perform many an antic jig. The wind picks up, the chimneysweeps wave good-bye, and she uses her new found Supergirl powers to ascend into heaven and assume geostationary orbit above the planet. She has the ghost of Yoda tucked under one arm like a football, and he blasts the Imperial battleships out of the sky in a trice with lightning bolts.

No, wait, that does not happen, even though, given what has already been established, it certainly could have. It is not any stupider than what does happen.

The trapped soldiers do not use their weapons to blast their way out. Instead, for no reason Mary Sue in the Millennium Falcon just so happens to land in an empty valley and she just so happens to finds the selfsame escape exit from the other side! Which she was not looking for and had no reason to believe was there!

And, having no knowledge of the situation, and no reason to believe that there is anyone on the other side seeking egress, she calls upon her training she never received from Master Mopey.

Remember when she said the Jedi had a magic power to enable them to lift heavy objects like rocks? And Master Mopey told her every word of what she just said was wrong? Well, putting this valuable lesson to use, she, um... uh... uses her magic Jedi power to lift the heavy rocks.

The Rebels are awed! They are saved!

They rush out the back door of the escape-proof base, enter a field of deadly rolling robot landmines, and are immediately blasted to bloody rags by the grim and battle-hardened veteran Stormtroopers of Spaceborne Deathsquad 1661, 'Lord Rancid's Roughnecks' who mined and cordoned off the area, in order to prevent any attempted breakout or sortie. Because surrounding a besieged location is what one does to besiege it. That is actually sort of the definition.

No, sorry, that does not happen, because the Imperial ground force is led by idiots, who do not do things like establish perimeters or proper air cover when besieging an enemy position.

Aboard the Millennium Falcon, the Rebels soar up into space, and, as they achieve orbit, are blown into fiery space-dust by the picket ships, cruisers, and corvettes the Imperial navy, who are not as stupid as the ground force, wisely deployed to throw a cordon around the planet, in order to prevent escape.

No, sorry, that does not happen, because instead the Empire uses the OMNITRON to track the Millennium

Falcon through hyperspace, intercepting the fleeing ship handily, and blasting her to atoms.

No, sorry, that does not happen, because instead, the Falcon races it to the Outer Rim, where there are no allies waiting for them. They hide on yet another rebel base, this time on a planet made entirely of pepper, and the Empire sends yet another flotilla to blow them up. The next movie can begin with the exact same word crawl without changing a syllable.

So, the whole movie consists of nothing happening.

Meanwhile, back on planet Swank, the slave children who muck the space stables are telling stories about the glorious cowardice of Master Mopey the Last Jedi, facing the Imperial tank squad while not really being there and accomplishing nothing, and how he was defeated for no reason. Through why the moppets would tell such a story is anyone's guess. Maybe they are telling a story of heroism and great deeds, the story this movie should have told.

The slavedriver bellows at them. One slaveboy steps outside, looks up at the stars, and, his heart now full of hope, puts out his hand, and uses the Force to levitate his pushbroom intro his grip, so that he can heroically and nobly go sweep up space-horse poop.

Yes, this nameless lad is destined to grow into none other than the great hero JEDI STABLEBOY!

Trumpet flourish! Roll credits! Then go burn down the theater in wrathful but misplaced retaliation for robbing you of perfectly good ticket money, not to mention robbing you of your childhood, and squandering your decades of hard-won loyal customer goodwill.

Have you, as so many of have, spent buckets, wheelbarrows, and dump-trucks full of money on Star Wars books, toys, games, accessories, clothing, comics, and multiple viewings of many films at the theater?

Is there any reason ever again to spend a single penny?

My ranting is not yet over. My spleen not vented. So far, we have only examined the story. Let us next turn to the fight choreography, character arcs, plot twists, themes that should have been in this film, and weren't. Let us also say what future these futuristic stories no longer have.

Along the way, we will see that what was given us instead of characters, plot, theme and potential for sequels was not just bad, but positively insulting to the spirit of Star Wars, and to the loyal customers. There is more than mere incompetence at work here.

12

THE NON-FIGHT SCENES

Let us pause to note for the final time how fetid, foul-smelling, malodorous, mephitic, noisome, noxious, putrid, stenchful, stinking, rancid and just plain bad each and every fight scene in this skunk bouquet of a film has turned out to be. Not just one fight scene, but each and every one has the same feminine tone.

Now here I have to talk about the difference between men and women, which is a topic forbidden to be discussed in the current political climate. I will confine myself to the obvious.

Here is what I mean: as anyone who has watched boys versus girls fighting can tell you, girls rarely enjoy the battle-frenzy of fighting, they are rarely good sports about it, and they do not understand chivalry.

In a chivalrous fight, you deliberately give up anything that might look like an unfair advantage, so that when you deck your foe, and you stick your hand out to help him up, he knows in his heart of hearts that you did not win by cheating, but just because you totally dominated him by skill and strength alone, and hence can easily destroy him, but choose not to.

He knows that if he does not accept your hand, you will destroy him. Chivalry, when extended to the loser, is meant to make him feel more helpless, and to force him to accept you no longer as an enemy, but now as a friend. (The friend is lower in the social hierarchy than the victor, but he is now in the hierarchy, and knows his place.) It is a simple survival mechanism used by gentleman and savage wolves alike to win both battles in the short term and wars in the long term. Chivalry is based on the idea this is not the last fight you will ever be in, because war will be with us, always.

Schoolboys play at fighting to learn how to control their strength and restrain themselves, so they can be brutal when brutality is called for, to knock heads together but save lives, or so they can be lethal when lethalness is called for, so they can kill quickly and efficiently with no hard feelings after.

Those who doubt me, if they do not know any schoolboys, can look at some of the Robin Hood ballads: see for yourself how often Robin has his ass kicked by Little John or Gamble Gold or Friar Tuck, who later become ale-friend or partners-in-crime or war-comrades.

No woman in his history of the world can ever really, truly understand this concept, not in her heart of hearts. Women, by and large, are created by nature and trained by custom to fight when and only when all retreat is cut off, all negotiation has failed, and there are little children cowering behind her, crying.

Then she fights like Mama Bear, and may use any trick or deception, any weapon, any blow fair or foul, feminine guile or human sadism can invent. And she is wise to kick the foe in his face when he falls, and slit his throat with the razor she uses to shave her legs, quickly before he finds his feet again. Because he is a monster, or else he would not have been fighting a woman to begin with.

Chivalry in the no-retreat save-the-children situation of a woman forced to fight would not merely be pointless, it would be counterproductive folly. Female battles are total war, and remorseless, without any Geneva conventions, because a woman is not likely to have the luxury of thinking in the long term. That is what the menfolk are for.

Suicide, however, has an allure to the female mind that chivalry does not. Thelma and Louise in their movie of the same name, please note, do not surrender to the police with a Burt Reynolds cocksure smile, saying, "Well played, officer! You nabbed me fair and square!" In the no-retreat save-the-children situation, a mother killing a monster at the price of her own life shows courage without parallel: like Christ for the faithful, she dies for her little ones.

In wars fought by men with men, however, it is more like a sporting event involving death and dismemberment. We follow the advice of Patton: "No dumb bastard ever won a war by going out and dying for his country. He won it by making some other dumb bastard die for his country."

Consequently, leftists and liberals, Jihadists, and other men who think in a womanish fashion or a barbaric fashion, cannot understand chivalry either. They do not enjoy fighting. And this comes over in stories they tell and movies they make.

None of the fight scenes in this sewer eruption of a movie show any zest, any seriousness, any tactics or cleverness, which is to say, any sportsmanship.

None of them are fun, except for the sour and limited fun of making fun of fight scenes, such as by having the robot KO the armored mooks by showering them with gold coins. That is a gag leading to a pratfall, not a boxing match, not a shoot out.

None of them have the edge-of-the-seat thrill even of a tied ballgame in the last inning, where each athlete is performing his utmost, every muscle rigid, every nerve straining.

Hotshot pilot in the first reel mocks his enemy with a prank call, showing the fight is not serious. Then he destroys all the hull cannons, showing the fight is totally one-sided. Then all the bombers butterfinger themselves to death, showing war is painful and pointless. Everyone dies. But then Hotshot saves the fleet from the fleetkiller dreadnought, and is demoted and slapped in the face. And on and on.

Ten Emo goes to shoot his mom with his mom-killing missiles. Boom. One and done. Tweedledim and Tweedledank are zoinked by traffic cops on Planet Swank. Zoink. Done. Mary Sue gets mad at Mopey Sulkwalker and knocks him on his buttocks. Done.

Throneroom guards assault two Jedi superhumans: mooks versus space wizards. No threat, no drama. Stormtroopers versus Billiard Ball: he mows them down with a walking tank like a farmer mowing hay. Done. Phasmid versus Tweedledim: she knocks him off a cliff without breaking a sweat, turns her back, and he is raised by *Deus Ex Machina* machinery literally back in place, cold-cocks her in a nasty, sneaky move unworthy of Gollum, and knocks her off a cliff in turn. It almost looked like a fight, but actually it is was two one-and-done fights, one immediately after the other.

Assault on the Salt Planet involves puny speedsters racing toward walking tanks, then breaking off because it is futile. Mary Sue flies through the glittering caves, shooting at clay pigeons. Superwoman versus mook pilots. No threat, no drama. No chance of victory, no drama. Every tank opens fire on Mopey the Jedi Master. Zoink and zoink. He steps out of the cloud of gunsmoke, looking casual. Almost a cool moment. Mopey and Emo duel, except not really. Nothing happens. He is not there. No threat, no drama.

Every fight scene is like this. Or, I should say, the fight scenes in this film aren't.

13

THE NON-CHARACTERS

C haracters in this film aren't.

A character is a pretend person, and has to act and think enough like a real person to seem realistic. A character can be simple or complex, as the genre and plot require, but he cannot be seen to have his personality change from scene to scene without some sort of under-standable cause , internal or external: an internal cause might be an intellectual realization, an emotional break-down, an attack of conscience; external causes involve the pressure of events.

More to the point, if the character is unchanged at the end of the tale as when the curtain rises, there is no char-acter arc. Normally, this is no problem for an adventure tale. James Bond, Sherlock Holmes or Captain Kirk is not expected to grow or change between episodes. But the orig-inal trilogy in Star Wars is a paramount coming-of-age story. Luke becomes a Jedi, Leia falls in love, Han goes from rogue to hero.

Who changes here?

MOPEY

Basically, the film-perp thought it would be a swell idea to insult, demean, humiliate, and break the character of Luke Skywalker, robbing fans of fond memories of the most beloved hero in sci-fi.

To do this, the film perp merely reversed every trait, ideal, and dream that Luke Skywalker stands for and fights for, and undid everything the experience, struggle, and growth we watched Luke suffer taught to him. All the hard-won wisdom we watched Luke achieve through in the first trilogy was thrown on the rubbish heap.

In the first trilogy, Luke is the optimist, the idealist, the starry-eyed youth who learns the shocking lesson that his own father is the Sauron of Outer Space, the evil, dark-hearted traitor in a skull-mask, Nazi helmet, black cape, and who sounds like an obscene phone call: a cyborg grotesquely marred, more machine than man, who cut down Luke's beloved master, Ben Kenobi, right before his eyes. The death of Luke's aunt and uncle was at Vader's orders. Luke is told Vader killed his father. Vader is the enemy who dismembered Luke when last they met, chopping off his sword hand.

In other words, Luke has every earthly reason to fear and hate Lord Vader, and no earthly reason to think any trace of good can still exist in the monster.

Luke defies the orders and ignores the wisdom of Ben and Yoda, who both tell him Darth Vader cannot be saved, and that there is no hope: he goes to Vader and says a spark of light yet lingers in him, that he still has faith. Luke can sense it when no one else can.

Even when standing before the throne of the evil Emperor, who might as well be Satan incarnate, Luke's pure faith allows him to drop his light-saber rather than raise it in anger against his father.

And his faith is answered: at the last minute, Vader remembers himself, sacrifices his life in an ultimate act of selfless love, and saves his soul, and dies redeemed. We see him glowing in Jedi heaven at the end of the film, even if his face changes depending on which version you watch.

So, in this abomination of a film, the film-perp decides that this is the character who in the meanwhile has reopened the old Jedi Academy, and is training new students. But then, for no particular reason, mystically sensing an unidentified evil rising in his own nephew and student, (a lad, please note, who has not, at that point in time, murdered anyone or maimed anyone) the old man decides to step into his student's bedroom and night and murder the child in his sleep.

Because redemption and reformation are impossible.

But since the Jedi Master is a total punk, and an incompetent, the child wakes, parries the blade, waves his hand, blasts the old man through the roof, and then burns down the school and kills or corrupts his other students.

And, to make him even more of a punk, we find out later that the Jedi Master had not really and truly been bending over the boy with the drawn weapon to kill him, that was just a mistake brought on by an instinctive reflex. Because the kid was so very, very evil, you know, and Jedi Masters do not practice controlling their emotions and reining in anger or anything.

The old man was just trigger happy. And also he is such a punk that the kid that his own student can parry him literally in his sleep.

Immediately coming to the firm conclusion that once a Jedi turns bad, there is no point either fighting him or redeeming him, and no way a fallen relative can ever find the light again, the old man then skips away to a remote

Irish monastery to sulk. But carefully leaves behind a map, so that if the galaxy ever needs him again, someone can come find him. The map was the McGuffin of the previous movie.

The character in that movie was willing to return to duty if needed. But then this movie says his motive is merely to dwell here in misery, despair, and remorse, until he dies. The character is this movie is unwilling to return to duty if needed. Conclusion: they are not the same character.

Instead of Luke, the man who turned Vader's heart away from the Dark Side, urging those who have lost hope to find it again, we have Mopey, who merely acts like a petulant and ill-mannered brat, sulking and sniveling, and who is afraid of Mary Sue's immense Force Powers, because she is so awesome, dontchaknow.

These are not natural and organic changes that might happen to a character after being mellowed by long years, or after being shocked by sudden tragedy. This is not taking a character in a new direction, nor is it exploring an aspect of his personality previously unexplored.

These are not changes at all. They are merely flat assertions that the previous character did not really act the way he acted. According to *Last Jedi*, Luke was not idealistic and brave, he was and is a self-pitying coward. He did not hold onto faith when all hope was lost, he was and is a bitter cynic, believing in nothing. He was not a Jedi Master, a sign of hope, or a great teacher. All that is illusion. The reality is that he is a vile old creep who sucks at the teat of an obscenely bloated green-milk-giving Dr. Seuss sea-cow.

The character arc was supposed to be: Mary Sue wakes Mopey out of his mopes like Gandalf restoring a warrior heart to Theoden, and he takes up his father's sword, finds his rusted fighterplane, and marches with his old comrade

Chewie and R2D2 into combat once more, there to lay down his life for his friends.

Instead, she annoys and pesters him and the audience, he refuses to go , he goes anyway for no reason, but not really. He stays safe at home, accomplishes nothing via interstellar astral illusion projection and dies anyway, again for no reason.

There is no character arc. He stands for nothing, accomplishes nothing.

GENERAL RUIN the SPACE WITCH

General Ruin has the same relation to Princess Leia as Master Mopey has to Luke Skywalker. I could dwell on what an abomination of this favorite and best-beloved character has been perpetrated, but the matter is almost too painful.

Princess Leia from Star Wars was spunky, indomitable, and yet vulnerable and feminine. She could shoot stormtroopers like a trooper and bark out order like a drill sergeant. No shrinking violet, this.

In this movie, General Ruin is old and tired. This is not necessarily the actress: this is the lines she was given to say, and how she was told to say them.

She is not indomitable: there is nothing parallel to the scene where she spits defiance to Grand Moff Tarkin to his face, or resists torture. The woman unwilling to surrender even after seeing her whole planet die, in this film is emotionally scarred by seeing a dozen ships and crews lost in combat.

But neither is she vulnerable, motherly, feminine. She conducts herself with a leaden-faced stoicism that seems particularly mannish.

There is a scene in *Empire Strikes Back* where Lando, having betrayed them, and, stung by regret, is trying to unbetray them, releases Chewie and Leia from their handcuffs. The hairy Wookie immediately starts strangling his old friend, while Lando frantically tries to convince Leia he is on the level. She is skeptical and rightly angered, and reads him the riot act.

Notice what she does not do. She does not slap him. She is not petty. Even in emergencies, she is still a princess. She is content to let an underling choke the scofflaw.

Now, the opposite. She is petty. She slaps subordinates, something a true princess would never, ever do.

In this movie, just as Luke is not a hero, Leia is not a heroine.

There is no emotional change or character change of any kind visible here. We neither see her regretting the downfall of her son, clinging to a false hope that he can be saved, and reluctantly coming to terms with the sad truth that he cannot be; nor do we see her, at first having come to terms with his downfall, finding unexpected and miraculous cause for hope again. Aside from one line, she does not talk about the boy at all, and it is easy for forget he is supposed to be her son.

There is no character arc here. She does nothing memorable. She has no personality.

THE TWEEDLE TWINS

These two characters are new, but nothing is done to establish their personality characteristics. Unless you consider 'craven' and 'manic depressive' to be character traits.

There is a simple rule of thumb any writer can use to see if his character has any personality.

Put his words in the mouth of another character, or imagine someone different doing the same action. If you can move the actions or lines around from character A to B without it being jarring or absurd, then the lines and acts are not sufficiently organic and innate to the character to make him seem real.

A similar rule of thumb works with changing the sex of the character. Call this the Twelfth Night test. If you can write the same scene with her as a man, or him as a woman, and their words and acts do not seem out of place, you do not know enough about men and women to be a writer.

There are exceptions, of course: in the military, in combat, words and actions are tightly controlled, and only the most broad of personality traits are visible. (Which is precisely why, in adventure stories, character nuance is left to one side.)

Dim and Dank do not pass the Twelfth Night test.

One example of many should suffice. Remember the scene where these two idiots first enter the swank casino of Swank Planet? He was impressed with the look of the luxury; she was scornful and scoffed.

Please imagine what happens if the two so-called characters in this scene were to swap lines.

Suppose the Wrench Monkey, who has never seen the high life before, is gushing over how grand and gilt the casino is, how pretty the dresses, and such, and the ex-Stormtrooper, a grim military man, says he recognizes these people as the arms dealers who sold illegal weapons to the Empire, and made their fortune from exploiting the war. Would anything else in the film need to change, if these lines were swapped?

Indeed, it seems to me the gushing would fit better with the woman, and the grim and focused comment with the man.

Try that trick with any two lines from the real *Star Wars*, and you will find that the Farmboy cannot swap lines with the Lovable Rogue.

Imagine Luke saying this: " Hokey religions and ancient weapons are no match for a good blaster at your side, kid." Hard to picture, eh? The writer and actor would have to change every aspect of this character from the beginning to make this line sound natural to him.

Or try, just try, to picture the sardonic and worldly-weary Han Solo rushing into the jail cell of the princess he has a crush on, and gushing: "I'm Han Solo! I'm here to rescue you!"

The words will not fit in each other's mouths.

Why? Because when a character is done right, he sounds like himself when he speaks.

Contrariwise, Dank and Dim do not sound like anything.

TWEEDLEDANK

Dank especially has no consistent voice or mood.

Dank is crying over her dead sister when the camera first finds her, and the scene should have been solemn in tone. Instead, in a jarring mood shift, Dank sees a man she hero-worships, and she is chattering and gushing over him like a schoolgirl meeting a rock star.

Then in the next mood shift, she is committing zoink on him, and blasting him across the cabin. Then a comedy scene of her shoving him around on a hand-truck, while he moans that his hands and feet are numb, while she snaps at him.

And then, just as suddenly, her face is lit up with excitement as she and he exchange lines of stupid technobabble while they, on the spot, using bat-logic, figure out the technical specifications and limits of the Imperial hyperspace radar tracking system.

Then comes the scene of them on planet Swank, of her scowling in righteous indignation like a Hellfire-Preacher condemning the rich and powerful at their leisure to the fate of Sodom.

Then we see her whooping in lighthearted childish joy as she rides a space-racehorse with her previously unmentioned jockey skills. Then she is sounding like a total self-satisfied idiot when she announces that freeing the race-horse from their comfortable lives as trained athletes to starve and freeze in the wild, or be eaten by the Sarlacc, is the only really worthwhile thing they risked their lives to do.

As for her quote about defeating the enemy not by fighting them, but by saving loved ones, this is so shallow, and so stupid, and so maddeningly smug and self-satisfied, that merely having the wounded character stepped on by the monster metal leg of an AT-AT would not have been revenge enough.

More to the point, this sudden pacifism (or whatever it is) is disconnected from anything that comes before.

The line, I assume, was meant to sound wise like Yoda, but this comedy relief dunderhead was not portrayed as having any insight or depth erenow. Her curtain line could have been given to any other character in the flick.

There is no character arc here, because she has no character.

TWEEDLEDIM

The promise made in *The Force Awakens* in that moment when we first saw Finn take off his helmet, and saw the face of a person, was startling. The promise was that a stormtrooper, who, up until now had been a faceless minion, no more human than targets in a shooting gallery, was going to be a main character, a man with a past and personality. He was to have hands, organs, dimensions, senses, affections, passions as any other character; fed with the same food, hurt with the same weapons, subject to the same diseases, healed by the same means, warmed and cooled by the same winter and summer.

I thought it was a bold move, because usually the mooks in a film do not even have names. When is the last time, for example, in a film by Chuck Norris or Jackie Chan, we ever saw a ninja with a broken collar bone slink away from a failed mass attack on our hero, and have to explain to his failure to his irate ninja master or his disappointed ninja wife clutching their weeping ninja child, and then see him, tempted by the demon of rice wine from his alcoholic days, put the bottle aside, try to find another gig in his dangerous line of work?

The idea of giving a stormtrooper a personality, and giving us an insight into the horrid inner workings of the Empire, had bucketloads of potential.

This idea was the *only* original idea from Disney. Everything else is just a politically correct do-over of the original trilogy. This character was the only one not merely a female version or Cuban version of a hero we have already seen done better three decades ago. Finn was new.

He could have been anything from a hardboiled cynic to a guilt-haunted defector to a starry eyed idealist to a pacifist vowing to fight no more forever. Heck, they could have even given him some Jedi training. That would have been something interesting. They could have made him as cool and cold-eyed as a Richard Roundtree character (for those of you old enough to remember him) or a wry-faced quip-cracking Will Smith character.

Originally, all the stormtroopers were clones. Having an ex-trooper decide to open fire on his own twin brothers, with whom he had been raised, would have also been quite dramatic. But even as a child-slave raised in bootcamp, his fellow troopers are the only family Finn has ever known. We should have at least seen a reaction shot the first time he sees, once in the outside world, a mommy and a daddy pushing a baby in a hover-pram or something.

Credit where credit is due: the moment in a elevator when a trooper recognizes Finn, now disguised in a stolen uniform, and thinks he made Captain, and gives him a friendly slap, actually was an endearing moment, or would have been, if it had been in a movie and in not in a shipwreck.

Imagine a character arc where, at first Finn is unwilling to use his knowledge of the passwords, communications, tactics and logistics of the Empire to help the rebels. He has been raised his whole life to believe the stormtroopers are invincible, so he is terrified of them; and he has heard nothing but propaganda about the rebels, and so thinks switching sides would be just a change of masters.

Then he learns betters, finds his heart and his courage, and faces down his old friends and leaders, especially his dreaded sergeant, for whom he has some affection as a father figure: this is the one who first taught him to field strip and clean a blaster rifle, after all, and saved his life during jungle-fighting on planet Stinkbag. (But the sergeant cannot be female: girl stormtroopers are silly.)

He fights and loses, licks his wounds and learns better, fights and overcomes the sergeant in the climax of his arc. After his enemy is down, Finn extends mercy, tells the older man of all the truths he'd learned, and extends his hand to his wounded mentor. The older man takes off his helmet then, and we see he, too, has a face.

The next scene shows the sarge now as a private in the rebel army taking orders from Sergeant Finn as they both prepare for an orbit-to-surface paratrooper drop to the fortress-planet where the major imperial base is hidden.

Or anything. Something. Instead we get nothing.

All that potential for drama from this bold move was wasted.

The character is played for laughs, gets zoinked and toted around by a dwarf woman like a comedy relief punching bag, is rescued *twice* by the Billiard Ball Bot, accomplishes nothing, shows no courage, no wits, no manliness. He does not even shoot a bounty hunter seeking him from under a table in a cantina to show that he is a cold-eyed killer, a cool as a cucumber. No, he wakes up wounded on a fleeing starship, and, at the film's end, is wounded in a fleeing starship.

Instead of a character arc, he has a skin color. He is a black spaceman. That is it. That is all he does. He has no other discernible characteristics.

Tweedledim was supposed to have a character arc, because the episode on Planet Swank should have shown him that the Empire was bad—something he actually knows better than any non-stormtrooper could possibly know it—and should have screwed his courage to the sticking place, and allowed him to commit the ultimate act of self-sacrifice when he rams the super-cannon and saves the rebel base.

But that character arc was zoinked away by the Wrench Monkey, for no reason.

MARY SUE

There is no character arc here, because she has no character. She has no expression throughout the movie aside from opening her mouth and opening her eyes. Her acting range reaches from an expression of self-righteous irritated surprise, to a self-righteous surprised irritation.

Allegedly, she should have been the hope of youth reminding the crusty old cynic, Master Mopey, of his long-forgotten ideals. She should have been the one who touches his heart, and stirs him to return to the fight, like Gandalf the Gray returning the heart of a fighter to Theoden of Rohan, or like the death of Uncle Ben reminding Peter Parker of the price of having great power.

Or, again, she should have been the light alluring the smothered conscience of Emo back to life, and drawing him toward the Sunny Side, as Luke was to Vader.

When a writer writes a scene where one character is trying to persuade or inspire another, the writer has to give the character making the speech enough depth, enough reality, to be able to imagine how the speech would be made: the character has to have a viewpoint, an approach, which makes his speech different from if someone else said it.

Since she is a Mary Sue, therefore perfect, she is a perfectly flat character with no background, no character, no driving force, and no personality, so, ergo, she actually has nothing to say to either character in either scene. She represents nothing because she is nothing.

Her character arc should have been parallel to Luke's, or to the archetypal hero of any hero's journey.

Luke's aunt and uncle are slaughtered, his home burnt. Luke sees his master cut down before his eyes; when he relies on the Force, he makes the thousand to one shot that blows up the Death Star; he is clobbered by snow-monsters and shot down by walking tanks; his copilot dies; he suffers absurdly strenuous training, including levitating rocks while performing one-handed handstands; he fails the moral test of the vision in the dark tree; he disobeys his master, fights his foe, and is overmatched, is maimed, and falls. Only then does he grow into mastery of the Force Force. He is tempted by the Emperor, and tormented with electric shocks. In the end, not by strength, but by mercy and faith does he prevail over his evil father, by finding and fanning in him the one spark of good no one else sees.

That is Luke's character arc. Mary Sue's should have been parallel, or, even if it had been a different arc, it should have been dramatic, engaging, interesting.

Instead her character arc is... nothing.

She knows everything about the Force with no training, and is also a better pilot than Han Solo, and a better mechanic, and an expert gunner.

Both Yoda and Mopey declare her to be a Jedi master even thought she knows nothing at all about the Jedi lore, and Yoda says she already has all the wisdom their holy books contain.

She fails at nothing, and loses no fights.

She can trash fully grown and trained stormtroopers with a stick, defeat a trained Sith killer the first time she touches a lightsaber, and knock a Jedi master on his buttocks in one pass of the blade. She saves the entire rebellion singlehandedly.

Her sole emotional problem was curiosity about her parents. But they turn out to be nothing and no one.

Instead of a character arc, she has a sex. She is female, but not feminine. She is a girl space-wizard. She has no other discernible characteristics.

HOTSHOT PILOT the MUTINEER

Not much to say about this character. In *Force Awakens*, he was supposed to be a pilot with the Right Stuff, and have the typical fighterpilot's devil-may-care bravery and charisma: he was supposed to be Maverick from *Top Gun*.

And they make him into a macho nitwit, or try to, except nothing he does is actually nitwittery. He is just a frustrated young man serving incompetent, self-centered, self-destructive, idiotic leadership.

If he had led just his squadron alone off in another direction at the beginning of the movie, he would have had more servicemen survive, and with better discipline and better chances of forming the kernel of a new rebellion than the clownboat of feminazi harridans, hags, and termagants driving the doomed Resistance to their certain deaths on the Salt Planet.

Whenever Hotshot came across Tweedledim, and gave him a brotherly hug, I had to pause to remember that those two had actually escaped together in the first movie, and so, in theory, they should have the grateful camaraderie of squad mates who have saved each other's lives. But they have had no screen time together, and hardly know each other.

Hence no camaraderie was established on screen. The film-perp wants to play off the emotion without taking the time to establish the emotion.

His character arc, if you can call it that, is that he gets humiliated for no clear reason by She-Admiral Hag, and then, later, again, by Space Witch. Instead of a character arc, he has a gender role: toxic male.

EMO VADER the SITH WANKER

Good grief. Even thinking about this character makes me want to get blind drunk, to climb into the bottom of a whiskey bottle and never come out again: and I am a lifelong teetotaler.

What is there to say about him? The reason why he turns evil is never given, his reason for serving the First Order is never clear, his motives are arbitrary, and change from scene to scene, and in one moment he is cool and calm, and in the next throwing hysterical temper tantrums like Gollum in a rage. Nothing makes sense.

SUPREME LEADER SNOOPY

Good grief. A bigger waste of potential cannot be envisioned. He, at least, unlike all the other characters, maintains a certain degree of consistency. He has a creepy voice and impressive stage presence. He dies a punk death.

With Snoke dead, the Empire is effectively leaderless (I dismiss Emo Vader without comment) they are no threat, and no source of drama. With Snoke dead, one of the driving mysteries is gone. Nothing is left to tickle audience curiosity.

Snoke apparently created Anakin Skywalker in his mother's virgin womb, like an evil space version of the Holy Ghost. What is his origin, that he commands such powers?

The answer is a slap in the face and a donkey laugh. There is no explanation, fanboy! Your Snoke theory sucks! Things happen for no damn reason from now on! Deal with it!

14

PLOT TWISTS AND PLOT PLOPS

Having reciting in excruciating detail every idiotic nuance of this dunderheaded plot, we can notice one thing is missing from the plot.

The thing missing from the plot is a plot.

The sad fact that nothing is at stake in this movie, and nothing matters, is obvious from the outset.

Yes, *bad guys chase good guys and good guys try to get away* should be a plot, but it was not, because the good guys did not really try to get away, and the bad guys did not really try to chase them.

Did the good guys make a successful escape? I cannot say they did.

By the end of this dog's breakfast of a film, the Resistance consists of one senile old lady on her deathbed, a hotshot pilot mutineer-cum-dogcatcher, a Mary Sue with magic space-witch powers, her pet Space Bigfoot, and a number of men so small that they can all fit aboard the Millennium Falcon. No allies in the Outer Rim are answering the calls for help.

The Resistance has proved itself to be incompetently

run, to be filled with soldiers as disciplined and devoted as the Three Stooges would be, if they were serving under Rufus T. Firefly.

Did their escape attempt fail? I cannot say it did not.

The only thing that preserves the Resistance from obliteration is the fact that the First Order consists of one flotilla of ships, six tank crews, one squad of stormtroopers, two comedy relief generals, one of whom dies, and two numskull evil space wizards, one of whom kills the other.

This clown parade of bumbling guards and bad shots is unmatched in slapstick bungling since the days of Sergeant Garcia from Disney's *Zorro* television show.

The Resistance, having dropped from four hundred to less than forty in a galaxy of millions of worlds, is in the same position at the end of the film as they were at the beginning: a small, hunted, pointless, worthless band of fugitives.

This pointlessness is present not just in the plot as a whole, but in every subplot, every scene, practically every action.

Nearly every thing any character attempts to do, fails miserably and comes to nothing, or ends abruptly and comes to nothing. It is as if the film-perp does not believe in the law of cause and effect.

I can think of only two lonely exceptions of times when someone actually does something he sets out to do and something actually comes of it: (1) Lord Snoopy luring Mary Sue into a trap, and (2) DJ Codebreaker betraying Tweedle twins. Except for Lord Snoopy, who dies a chump death pointlessly while in mid-rant.

So only once does anyone accomplish anything: DJ Codebreaker gets away with his Judas money. (I hope to see

DJ and the Jedi Stableboy in Episode IX being hunted down by the ruthless yet faceless Imperial fighterpilot XPIOI.)

Now, it may be objected (by what or whom, I cannot imagine) that this film deliberately intends to subvert viewer expectations, much like George R. R. Martin killing off the character you thought would grow into the avenging hero, and that therefore the inability of this film to have any plotlines bear fruit is a feature, not a bug.

The argument might be made that these are not examples of bad writing, but gotcha! moments when the film-perp playfully yet impishly yanks the rug out from under the feet of the ticket-buying public, and then laughs at them with a braying donkey-laugh, glorying in their anger and disappointment.

So, if that is the argument, let us review the events in the film:

Hotshot pilot goes nose-to-nose with a space dread-naught, and is sure to die but instead he is only there to blow up the hull guns to clear a path for the bombers! Gotcha! But the bombers are destroyed anyway! Gotcha! But one bomber is still flying! Gotcha! But it cannot drop its bombs because butterfingers the pilot is dead. Gotcha!

But attractive Vietnamese actress climbs up the latter to get the remote control, but she falls to her doom. Gotcha! But she is still alive! The remote falls down in space and she fails to catch it! Gotcha! But she caught it anyway! She drops the bombs! Gotcha! But then she dies! Gotcha!

But Hotshot is told to break off the attack, and he disobeys a direct order. So instead of being a hero, he is demoted! Gotcha!

Mary Sue meets the heroic legend, Luke Skywalker, and proffers him his lightsaber. He tosses it over his shoulder as if it were trash. Gotcha! And he is not Luke Skywalker; he is

Mopey Sulkwalker! Gotcha! He will not help her! Gotcha! But then he says he will train her, but then he doesn't! Gotcha! And he is responsible for creating Kylo Ren, whom he tried to murder in his sleep as a child! Gotcha!

Emo Vader cannot blow up his Mom with his evil Mom-killing missile! Gotcha! She gets blown up anyway by faceless pilot XP101 who is offscreen! Gotcha! But then she does not die, but uses an unmentioned previously-unguessed magic power to fly back home. Gotcha! But then, even though she is telekinetic, she never uses this power again, nor is it mentioned.

Mopey, instead of being a good teacher loyal to his tradition, wants to end the Jedi and blow up the Jedi sacred library. Gotcha! But Mopey cannot blow up the Jedi library. Gotcha! Yoda appears out of nowhere and does it instead. Gotcha! Except the books were stolen by Mary Sue for no reason and out of no motivation. Gotcha! And she is already so wise she does not need them!

Tweedledim is going to steal a spaceboat and abandon the Rebel fleet. You thought he was a hero. Gotcha! But then he is zoinked by Dank. Gotcha! But then he goes on a spy mission and is zoinked by meter maids. Gotcha!

In jail there is a sleazy guy, who turns out to be a master codebreaker. Gotcha! They escape but are cornered by the cops. Gotcha! But are saved for no reason by the codebreaker who has no reason to be in that spot, no way to know they were there, and no motive to help them. Gotcha!

So, they sneak aboard the flagship and accomplish less than nothing, since they walk into a trap. Gotcha! The codebreaker tells the Empire the rebel flotilla escape plan, which he only discovered because the morons discussed it in front of him. Gotcha! And the escape plan is ... wait for it ... use spaceboats and abandon the rebel fleet. Stupid!

Then Finn shows a self-sacrificing heroism as he dives headfirst toward the bore of the super-cannon, and you realize he has overcome his cowardice, and will die a hero. Gotcha! But then Tweedledank rams his speeder with hers, and shoves him out of the way, in order to steal a kiss from him. Gotcha! And, as she is stealing a kiss, the rebel base in the background is clobbered by a vast explosion! You moron! And she dies! Good!

But then he drags her fat ass across the salt flats to safety! Which is absurd, because both are in plain view of the tank crews while struggling slowly across a flat landscape with no cover and no concealment! So Dank is not dead as she should be, but alive to face a court martial! Gotcha!

Mary Sue goes to save Emo, but is arrested instead. Gotcha! Their mental link was a trick by the Grand Muppet Snoopy. Gotcha! But then Emo does an about face and turns good and kills Snoopy. Gotcha! But then he does a double about face and he is still evil. Gotcha!

Emo and Mary Sue are blasted off their feet when Luke's lightsaber explodes, but Mary is somehow perfectly fine and departs from the damaged ship without being seen or caught. Gotcha! Then on the Salt Planet, Mary Sue pops up out of nowhere, and blasts three enemy ships in one go, even though she has never worked as an antiaircraft gunner before. Surprise!

And then she immediately leaves the battlefield, and does not open fire on the siege gun, because, uh, something something, and the rebel base doors get blasted open by the enemy! Gotcha!

But then Master Mopey is not a quitter after all, but has come to save the day! Surprise! And then he is shot to bits by every single tank gun in the tank squad, except, Gotcha! He walks out of the smoke cloud of the gunfire, brushing a speck of dust off his shoulder. Cool!

Emo goes to face him and cuts Mopey neatly in half with one stroke of the lightsaber! Except, Gotcha! Mopey is a magical hologram projected across interstellar distances, so he is not really there at all! Ergo he cannot be killed! Except, Gotcha! He dies anyway and for no apparent reason! Gotcha! Before he dies, he tells Emo that there is one last Jedi!

Yes, you fools, he means Mary Sue, the one girl who needs no training for anything! You were expecting something to make sense? Gotcha!

Hotshot realizes that the escape proof hideout must have a backdoor, or else how else did Mopey get in? Gotcha! There is no backdoor, because Mopey is a hologram!

But the space fox got in, so they follow the critter back to a hole too small to crawl through. Gotcha! But then Mary Sue waves her hand and clears the tunnel of the boulders! Everyone gets away! Happy ending! And the stableboy back on Planet Swank is now a Jedi! For no reason! Nothing happens for any reason! Gotcha! Gotcha!! *Gotcha!!!*

You expected Luke to be a hero and a legend, because he slowly and painfully gained that stature in the original trilogy. But here, he is shown to be a dimwitted, emotionally inconsistent, utterly foolish, griping coward. Gotcha!

You expected Grand Muppet Snoopy, a Sith more powerful than Vader or Palpatine, to have a backstory and have some meaning. Gotcha!

You expected Mary Sue's search for her parents to have a payoff. Gotcha!

You expected drama, cleverness, emotional weight, that a well-told story would have? You expected character development, thematic consistency, and a respect for the original source material that you love and adore? Gotcha! Gotcha!! *Gotcha!!!*

Within the many-tentacled mess of this random, loopy nonsense, what is missing? Why are these not perfectly cromulent plot twists meant to subvert viewer expectations?

Let me state, as a professional writer, one of the simplest and hardest lessons of the craft of writing. Rian Johnson has been making films about half a decade less than I have been selling novels, so I hope the reader will grant me that I might know something about the craft.

A plot twist is not the same as a plot plop.

A plot twist is when an unforeseen turn of events leads to a satisfying payoff, but it makes sense in hindsight.

A plot plop is when an unforeseen and unforeseeable event stumbles into a chain of events, breaking the chain, so that some other thing happens, but no one really cares, because there is no pay off. Expectations are cheated. The Christmas present so brightly wrapped in so much gay ribbon turns out to be an empty box.

Now, it is surely and certainly true that a plot plop is unexpected. If I go to a high class Italian restaurant, and there is a dead toad in my minestrone soup, I honestly did not expect that. And if, upon voicing a polite but firm complaint to the dark-haired Sicilian waiter, he yanks a flask of pressurized industrial-strength cheez-whiz out of his tool-belt, and squirts it painfully up my left nostril, filling my sinus cavities with yellow dairy-product-flavored goo, I will honestly and truly say I did not expect that as well.

Whereas if the chef had added chickpeas or chili oil to the soup for extra zest, instead of a toad, would also be a surprise, this would be a variation on the standard recipe, without destroying the soup. And the waiter is much more likely to get a fat tip in such a case.

The events in this film do not grow logically if unexpectedly out of preceding events, and none have the satisfying end-result the paying customer has a perfect right to expect from the recital of events in a story.

In a word, point of storytelling is that the events recited have a point, a payoff. But no point means no story.

Remember the blind cutpurse who steals the bag but leaves the coin?

A plot plop is an attempt to subvert expectations by the mere idiot trick of having something happen that is stupider and less satisfying that what a paying customer with normal tastes has a perfect right to expect. A plot plop is something disconnected from previous events, or utterly out of character, prompted by no established motive, happening for no reason.

A plot twist adds meaning, drama, and satisfaction to a plot by the sheer delight of the unexpected, but, more to the point, the event makes more sense, not less: there has to be a set-up and there has to be a payoff.

A plot-plop subtracts all these things, it disappoints; it cheats expectations; and there is no payoff.

Let one example serve for many. Take the scene where, out of nowhere and for no good reason, when Hotshot the Dogcatcher politely asks his commanding officer for instructions, to know what the battleplan is so he can prep his men, and so on, the Purple-Haired Hag browbeats and humiliates him in a lecture that consists of sneers and accusations. She answers his perfectly understandable question with hatred and contempt.

Unexpected, yes, but it is not a plot twist.

It is such a jarring note, so out of place in a heroic space-adventure film, so absurdly unlike how military personnel generally are required to conduct themselves, that it stands out like a toothache. (Or, it would stand out, if the rest of this film atrocity were not just as bad. One cannot see the polar bear against the snow, after all.) Putting aside the emotional tin-eared tastelessness of having such a scene in an adventure film, the scene is inept writing.

By inept writing, I mean a violation of the most basic rule of storytelling.

Let me put this simply: stories are make-believe. The events are not really happening, but someone, namely the writer, is deciding that they happen and he decides the order in which they happen. But he has to make the events seem to be real, at least insofar as the willing imagination of the audience is concerned.

The prime thing we notice about events in the real world is cause and effect. Nothing comes out of nothing for no reason, and nothing goes into nothing for no reason.

But the events in the make believe world come about because the writer says so, but he has to make it look to the willing imagination of the audience as if the events are natural, coming from somewhere for a reason, and leading to something. The thing that makes it a story (and not a pretend news report) is that the events also need to have a point, to carry some emotional weight, and to lead to a satisfactory culmination of the expectations.

Hence, the events in a story have to be *set up* before they happen, and have a *follow-through* after they happen.

In this case, the reptilian enmity of Purple Hair toward Hotshot is not foreshadowed in anything coming before, nor is there a come-uppance nor follow-through where the hag learns the error of her ways. If anything, it is clear that the film-perpetrator took it for granted that the audience should side with the hag automatically.

It must be emphasized that while this looks like utter incompetence in film making, it is not.

Every jarring note and brainless plot hole is a product of policy. The writer-director here also made *Brick*, a superb film-noir style murder mystery ironically set in a high school setting.

He is not incompetent, or, rather, he knows how to not be incompetent, but is willing to sacrifice that knowledge, to ignore it, for the sake of a policy.

The policy of a story is what we call a theme: the emotional meaning of the events and the characters is the theme, the coherent worldview in which such events and characters make sense.

In this case, the policy of the story is to say that no consistency motivates actions, actions do not have necessary consequences. There is no virtue, no truth, no logic. Kill the past.

This is called nihilism, the philosophical posture that there is no objective reality, only propagandistic narratives that serve the self-interest of powerful factions.

The treason of Rose Tico is not the sole nihilist moment, merely the culmination of a series of them, imposed, if I am not mistaken, not by mischance or through ineptitude, but due to a philosophy that regards the honest enjoyment of loyal customers for a tale of simple heroism as a disgusting self indulgence which must be undermined, mocked, and annihilated. Kill the past.

In a fantasy science fiction story, there is a second layer of consistency aside from plot consistency needed for the audience to retain its suspension of disbelief in the story: even in the midst of the wildest magic, and most unexpected events, even in a world utterly different from our own, the logic of the world has to stay consistent with itself.

Even the magicians can only do what they are established to be able to do.

In this case, there are so many violations of world-building consistency that I doubt my power to list them all.

The most obvious is the scene where one ship rams another at lightspeed, but no reason is given to explain why this maneuver had not been known and performed since the dawn of space combat. The prior movies make it clear that a ship in hyperspace flies outside three-dimensional space, hence is immune from all outside interference, and hence unable to effect nor be affected by any sub-light object.

I, myself, or any other half competent hack writer, can think of fan-save explanations to save the appearances, and some of them would only have taken an extra moment, and extra line, to put in. Ask yourself why such a line is missing.

The second most obvious is that, despite the lengthy training sequence we see Luke suffer in *Empire Strikes Back* in order to learn how to use the Force, in this flick, anyone and everyone can use the Force without training, from Mary Sue to Luke's untrained sister to a slaveboy who shovels spacehorse droppings.

Other violations of the science fiction continuity arguably include the plethora of new Force powers unseen erenow, and growing naturally out of no prior use: (1) a ghost pulling lightning out of the sky; (2) flying unharmed like Mary Poppins through hard vacuum; (3) projecting illusions across an interstellar distance, including illusions with physical solidity, as when Han Solo's dice are placed in his widow's hand; (4) linking two minds so that they receive mutual mental hologram calls from each other; (5) teleporting at least some physical matter across interstellar distances via mutual mental hologram calls, as when Emo has a raindrop on his hand shed by Mary Sue, who, on her planet, was in the rain; (6) poking the living with a stick after you are dead, as the ghost of Yoda does to Mopey; (7) cutting yourself off from the Force and also; (8) using the Force to reconnect yourself to the Force when you had been disconnected and do not have any Force powers, including this one; and (9) the ability, used by Emo just before he backstabs his Sith master, to deceive a telepath while he is reading your thoughts, so that he misunderstands your intent.

Of these, only the first has any arguable in-story precedent: evil Sith Lord Palpatine could throw forked bolts of energy from his fingertips, and so could Count Dooku. Neither could actually command nature to produce lighting from a clear blue sky. But it is not beyond belief that an expert at the one could perform the other.

Finally, the one Force power that invalidates and makes absurd the whole Star Wars universe and everything in it, is (10) the balancing power, where the Force, apparently as an automatic, unthinking process, will bestow full-blown master-class Jedi powers on random nobodies equal and opposite to Sith powers learned through long hours of disciplined training.

Presumably the opposite is also true, and Sith users crop up out of nowhere, like Anakin's virgin birth, whenever Jedi get too powerful.

This means the war between the Force and the Dark Side is eternal and unwinnable. The wars in Star Wars can never end and can never have any point.

15

NON-THEME OF NO-EMPOWERMENT

I n storytelling, there are four types of consistency needed.

A caveat before beginning: these comments are not meant to define an absolute rule. Consistency in storytelling is like a little bird in the hand. If you hold your fist too tightly, the little bird dies. If too lax, the little bird escapes.

Perfect and ironclad consistency is not required. The readers will allow a degree of unrealistic leeway for artistic exaggeration, irony, drollery, coincidence, dramatic effect, or to get the hero out of a tight spot.

Also, certain genres also have different expectations. Traditionally, Hard SF is allowed to violate no known principles of science (except, of course, for faster-than-light drive) but characters are allowed to be less realistic. Likewise, Space Opera does not care twelve parsecs for scientific accuracy, but insists the heroes act consistently heroic. Flash Gordon can never be portrayed as a scoundrel, liar, coward, or a womanizer.

With these exceptions in mind, let us contemplate the four consistencies storytelling needs:

One, the make-believe people must act like real people, that is, the pretend people must have a character and stay in character. Even when they grow or change or do something unexpected, they have to do it in the way that particular make-believe person would do it, and no one else in the story. In other words, all characters must act in character even when acting out of character.

Two, the make-believe events happen because the story-teller so arranges them, but the events must not look like events deliberately arranged. They must look as real events would look naturally arising from what has gone before, and naturally leading to their consequences. In a story, the events must have a point. In other words, all events must have set up before they happen, a point once they happen, and any natural follow through after they happen.

Three, the make-believe world has to act like a real world, even if its laws and habits are not real. The make-believe laws of the world must be true to themselves.

This is especially true in fantasy and science fiction, where things happen under laws of nature unlike ours, or with scientific understanding unlike ours: hence things which could not happen in our world must be made to act as they would act were they real.

Science fiction writers especially have to be careful. So, for a science fiction writer, if pigs had wings, the farmer's pigsty would have a roof like a dovecote to prevent the pork from flying off over the neighbor's hedgerow. The piglets would be trained with lure, leash, hood, and jesses like a falcon to return at the swineherd's call.

No matter how ridiculous or playful the premise is that pigs have wings, the logical effects and side-effects of such a premise must be carried through with perfect seriousness.

Likewise, fantasy writers have to be careful not to violate

the mood. Laws of aerodynamics they can take or leave, but the bat-winged demons and butterfly-winged fairies who fly have to fly right. If the fairytale reality is touched by the least smidgen of cynicism and skepticism, the fantasy is no longer fantastic: you have instead a satire, or a melodrama, a tragedy, or a historical romance where, for some reason, some of the crooks or kings have weird powers.

But now we turn to the fourth and final consistency all stories must have to be stories: a theme, a worldview, a consistency of tone.

Even in a story where the tones are mixed, such as when the comedy in *Ghostbusters* is mixed with horror elements, the mixed tones find the harmonic chord. This is not the same as having tones jar and contradict each other.

And even in a tale where tones are mixed, the overall tone of the work, its theme, must be steady. The theme and message of *Ghostbusters* is present in every scene: it is a typically American success story of small businessmen being hounded by intrusive bureaucrats, in their case, the EPA, and rising to be heroes despite all. There is not one slam nor sneer against self-reliance, risk-taking, advertising, or money making anywhere in the film: such a joke would not fit.

Contrariwise, there is no tonal and no thematic consistency even scene by scene in *Last Jedi*.

We open with a comedy routine of Hotshot mocking Admiral Unthreatening. A comedic note. Then we see horrific and tragic deaths of the bomber crews, including Rose Tico's attractive sister, Veronica Ngo. A somber note. Then Rose is crying: an unearned hence empty bit of pathos, since the sister was on stage for but an eyeblink, and spoke no lines.

A moment later, a slapstick note intrudes as Tweedledim

wakes in the infirmary and falls out of bed. This lame comedy is followed by the lame comedy of a coward who is thought to be a hero stammering out his lame excuses to a zoink dwarf. Then he is zoinked, and falls on his butt. Then more lame slapstick is shoved up the nostrils of the audience.

Then Dim and Dank go on a mission, and it is supposed to be serious and grim again: ooh! All those awful rich people! Free the ponies! Support PETA! Then more lame moral posturing is shoved up the nostrils of the audience.

But Billiard Ball shoots Chuck-E-Cheese tokens at the traffic cops and knocks them out. Comedy gold!

Then we see old hag slapping young Hotshot pilot for being too hotshot. Masculinity is toxic. Heroism is toxic.

Then we see Mopey Sulkwalker toss his famous weapon, his Excalibur, contemptuously over his shoulder. Heroism is a fraud. The Jedi, whom everyone in the audience knows are good and chivalrous men, are now bad men, and their books and memory must be expunged with fire.

Then Girl-General Gender Studies commits suicide to save her comrades, and that is good; but when Finn tries the exact same thing one reel later, that is bad.

Then more stupid happens.

The humor in *Last Jedi* breaks the tone of the drama into which the idiot slapstickery intrudes, just as the somber moments jar the humorous. This is more than the discord of two instruments in a band being out of key: more like two instruments in the band playing a jig and a dirge overtop each other.

It would be different if even one of the jokes were funny. None were. It would be different if any of the morals were actually in keeping with real moral truth. None are. It would be different if any of the thrills actually contained any moment of real danger, or any of the mysteries provoked even the slightest curiosity. None do.

The theme is nothing. Nothing means anything. It is shown in every plot-plop, emphasized at every turn, and even spoken aloud by the sockpuppets to the audience: kill the past.

What do you think 'kill the past' means?

It means all the triumphs and lessons painfully learned before, all the growth, all the value of everything remembered, is now set at naught. Nothing you did in a prior movie means anything. None of those movies mean anything. The Star Wars universe means nothing.

That is what 'kill the past' means.

That is what 'it is time for the Jedi to end' actually means. It is time for the Star Wars franchise to end. That is what the film-perpetrator is saying with this film.

It is not a hidden message, nor a subtle one.

There is no consistency of theme between this film and anything else in prior films, books, comics, games, or other source materials. In the whole rest for the Star Wars universe, there is no room for nihilism, because nihilism is not merely unheroic and unhopeful, it is anti-heroic. It is numb despair. By intruding into *Last Jedi*, this numb and anti-heroic worldview makes a mockery of all that has gone before.

What is being presented in all this badly written mess is a vision, a worldview, and a moral message: and that is the message of modern nihilism, which says every one makes his own truth for himself.

It is the message of self-centeredness, as when Rose Tico commits her treason for selfish reasons: to save a man she is crushing on.

This film teaches that nothing matters, nothing is worth

doing, all heroes are false, all legends are lies, all heroes are cowards. Masculinity is toxic; the Force is female; Wealth is theft. Good is evil and evil is good.

Now, as a film, it is clear enough that this is a dumpster fire and a failure in every element of storytelling: plot, characterization, world-building, and theme.

Events happen for no reason and come to nothing. Dramatic situations are deliberately undermined into boring and pointless waste-motion. Characters do not stay in character. There is no consistency of tone. Nothing has a point nor payoff.

Whole scenes are irrelevant, a clot of confused events having nothing to do with anything before or after. Periodic eructations of political correctness intrude into the proceedings, as welcome as flatulence at a wedding mass.

In a stand-alone film, these flaws would be damning. But this is Star Wars. The whole point of Star Wars is to be an update of a 1940s space adventure serial: Buck Rogers with modern special effects.

Other films have sequels or prequels. This is a serial. Serials have episodes.

Therefore this episodic structure imposes an extra demand on the filmmaker. In a serial, not only must the film be consistent internally and externally, that is, each episode must be properly fitted into its place in the overall story arc.

Unlike other stories, in a serial, the story is larger than any one episode. The set-up plot points in prior episodes must be given a satisfactory pay off in the current one. Likewise, the plot points of subsequent episodes must be set up in the present.

Serials have something no other form of storytelling has: respect for tradition. By this I mean only that in the same way, in a traditional society, the current generation both honors ancestors with gratitude and passes along the legacy due posterity with scrupulous honesty, so too in a serial the current episode remembers and honors the set-up done in prior episodes, and carries through on their promise to the subsequent episodes.

Now, as best I can tell, there are rabid shills ready, willing, and eager to defend this movie and the decisions of the film-perpetrator.

Those shills attempting to defend *Last Jedi* on two grounds:

First, they say how original and daring it is to violate the expectations of all the other films.

Second, they say it is artistically and perhaps even morally wrong of the fanboys, hence shallow, to yearn for the nostalgia of the older films to be seen again. Grow up, take your medicine, and learn to enjoy a bitter and cynical dismissal urinating on all childhood hopes and dreams. It is time for your Mom to throw away your comic book collection!

The perpetrators of the first argument, if any are so foolish as to make it, base their argument on a misunderstanding.

It is no merit to be daring and original in the middle episode of a trilogy, not if, as here, it means leaving the points set-up in the prior episode hanging with no resolution (as in Snoke's backstory, or Rey's parents), or if it means, as here, neglecting the next episode, and setting up no plot points, nor mystery, nor romance, nor tension, and, in a word, having nothing that need be resolved in episodes to come.

Let me quickly list the things *Force Awakens* set up for resolution or development in this flick, which, instead, were summarily dismissed without explanation or follow through.

SETUP: Lord Snoopy, erenow seen only as a shadowy giant, scarred from unknown wars, commanding unknown powers, has erected the First Order, complete with planet-sized sun-killer weapons, fleets of battleships, and legions of stormtroopers, but where and how all this power arose is yet to be explained.

FOLLOW THROUGH: He is killed off in a one-and-done chump death. Nothing explained. Nothing matters.

SETUP: The students Kylo Ren seduced to the Dark Side become the Knights of Ren; Kylo's dons a strange mask; he grows obsessed with his grandfather Vader, to whom he prays as to a pagan god. Vader is said to have unfinished business. Some echo or ghost of evil power in the Dark Side has informed Kylo, and he vows to see his grandfather's evil plan to the end.

FOLLOW THROUGH: His knights are never mentioned. Kylo's previously cordial Sith master, suddenly acting out of character, mocks the mask as childish in public. The mask gets smashed. Vader's unfinished business is unfinished yet. Nothing explained. Nothing matters.

SETUP: Luke Skywalker vanished for a mysterious reason, possibly to the mystic, legendary planet of the original Jedi temple, leaving behind a map in two pieces, one with R2D2, one with Max von Sydow, to give his friends a way to find him should he again be needed.

FOLLOW THROUGH: He came to planet Mopey to mope and die. The map is not explained. It does not matter. Nothing matters.

SETUP: Anakin Skywalker's lightsaber, saved by Ben Kenobi but lost by Luke when he fought Dark Helmet in Floaty City, is in the bar of the candy-corn-colored barkeep.

FOLLOW THROUGH: It is tossed off a cliff. Nothing is sacred. Nothing matters.

SETUP: Mary Sue's family, whom we saw as scattered images, and her origin, possibly will explain how she comes to be so absurdly powerful in the Force, and what her role might be. A daughter of Palpatine, perhaps?

FOLLOW THROUGH: She is nobody, sold into child's slavery for drinking money. Her parents are dead. Nothing explained. Nothing matters.

SETUP: *With the support of the REPUBLIC, General Ruin Ourtale leads a brave RESISTANCE.* They seek safe harbor with their allies in the Outer Rim territories.

FOLLOW THROUGH: The Resistance, after destroying the sun-eating planet, consists of three medium-sized spaceships. All are destroyed. There are no allies. Everything for which all the heroes fought and died is gone. Nothing matters.

SETUP: Finn had his spine broken protecting Mary Sue. Apparently they share some special bond or destiny. He is willing to abandon his post while under fire to seek her out and see to her safety.

FOLLOW THROUGH: What injuries? What special bond? Nothing matters.

SETUP: The First Order is the Empire come again. They are evil. The Resistance is the Rebellion come again. They are good.

FOLLOW THROUGH: Neither Emo Vader nor Mary Sue are either good or evil. Instead, everyone buys weapons from arms dealers on Swank Planet, who beat their space racehorses and keep child slaves. No one is right. No one is wrong. Nothing matters.

This is not even a complete list.

Orphaning every plot point is not daring. Deflating a tire

is not daring, it just prevents the automobile from moving smoothly.

It is not even original, not in the proper sense of the word. It is unusual in the sense that most writers do not deliberately wreck their own works by spitting in the face of the rules of writing, nor in the face of the fandom.

What it really is, is negligent. It is neglect, perhaps deliberate neglect, of the duty the middle episode owes the past and future episodes. If you are episode two of a trilogy, 'kill the past' is the stupidest and most wicked strategy imaginable to tell a story. As if one chapter in the middle of a twelve-chapter storybook should mutiny.

Their second argument (as best I can tell) boils down to a murky and satanic desire to see woe inflicted on fanboys, whom the shills dismiss as being nostalgic for the unrecoverable past.

If there is a worse, shallower, or sillier argument under heaven, I am blissfully unaware of it.

First, such an argument is *ad hominem*, therefore irrelevant. A man who had never seen or never liked any prior films could clearly count the plot holes larger than canyons, be bewildered by the inconsistent tone of the characters, be annoyed by the film's addiction to idiotic gotcha moments, hear the bad music, see the wooden acting, and smell the putrid theme of nihilism and loathing seeping from this crock.

Second, from the first moment of *Star Wars*, where the words promise a story from long ago and far away, and a word crawl, something not seen since the serial chapter-plays of *Buck Rogers* and *Flash Gordon* from the 1940s, the tone of nostalgia is set.

This franchise is meant to be nostalgia, and always has been.

Even in the day when I first saw *Star Wars*, and it was a single, stand-alone film with no sequel even dreamed-of, it was meant to conjure up the solemn silliness, and space fairytale feeling, of Buck Rogers and Flash Gordon.

This is not Stanley Kubrick and Arthur C. Clark with their eerie meditation on the shape of human evolution; this is not even Gene Roddenberry or John W Campbell Jr. with their Space Race optimism and wry social commentary. This is certainly not Mary Shelly or Aldous Huxley and like with dire warnings of science run amok.

This was pure-quill, one hundred proof Space Opera hokum, heavy on the cheese, bring on the Space Princess, and blow up the planet with a bang.

The first movie from the first moment of the first word crawl was meant to hearken back to childhood afternoons at the matinee, watching Spy Smasher pummel Nazis, or Flash Gordon thwart the sinister plans of Ming the Merciless, or the Gene Autry and the kids of Radio Ranch fighting the subterranean super-science of the Phantom Empire.

This film and all that followed were wildly successful because, by some magic, even those of us not old enough to recall the days of nickel matinees and the cliffhanger serials, are somehow aware of them.

Certain images and archetypes seep into the mass subconsciousness, so we do not need to be told why villains wear black capes, wise old wizards wear hoods, who the Evil Empire is, what it means when a smuggler in a smoke-filled cantina set in a wretched hive of scum and villainy shoots a gangster from under the table, or why one must rescue a beautiful Space Princess. Somehow, in the forgotten memories of childhood, we all know these things.

No one takes them seriously. Yet, in a mysterious way, they are the most serious things of all.

Star Wars and all that followed achieved fame precisely because Star Wars rejected the cynical and smirking cynicism and faux moral pharisaism of films so popular among the artiste elite of the time.

The artiste elite still hate the Star Wars franchise and everything about it. Optimism is an American spirit. The elite do not like it. Depressed and dispirited peoples are easier to frighten and to rule, and easier to form into mobs.

The shills no doubt like this movie precisely for the same reason we dislike it: it is Anti-Star Wars.

Let us turn finally to the last question of propaganda. It is a question in two parts.

Part one of the question asks whether this movie was a good vehicle for promoting the worldview of nihilism, despair, self-loathing, and political correctness that possesses and fascinates the warped minds of the modern Leftwing elite?

The question answers itself. I can think of no strategy that would be more adroit or more clear to show the shortcomings of nihilist worldview, the unpleasantness of its partisans, than to attempt to use Star Wars as a vehicle of nihilist propaganda. Everything in the background and foreground is diametrically opposed to the attempt.

In the foreground are the characters, who are unironically and unapologetically heroic and strong.

Nihilism, in its modern form, says that woman cannot be strong and be feminine. In order to be strong, she must be a man, and therefore men must be children, hence incompetent, pathetic, toxic, brutal, stupid.

But Star Wars has Princess Leia, who is both strong and feminine, and she need never throw a punch. Star Wars has Luke Skywalker, who becomes a Jedi Knight, and therefore is strong both physically and, what is more rare, spiritually:

he is heroic but also gentle and wise, willing to throw his lightsaber away rather than strike at his fallen father. No thug he.

Even the handsome brute Han Solo, who shoots a bounty hunter to death underhandedly (and, yes, he shot first) learns that the cynical worldview of world-weariness he thinks is wisdom is hollow and unsatisfying. He becomes a hero, and a leader, and a lover, and a family man. He is as manly as they come, but only a harpy could call his masculinity toxic.

In Star Wars, as in all true tales, the power of the heroes, even when they are weak, is because they have the moral authority of goodness. Whether they are physically strong enough to win or not, their purity grants them that they ought to win.

This authority is so strong that even when a *deus ex machina* is required to lower a god via stage machinery and let the heroes win against all odds, other considerations are put aside: Luke, aided by the blessing of a ghost whose voice only he hears, shuts off his targeting computer and makes the million-to-one shot that blows up the otherwise invulnerable ogre-castle in space of the Death Star.

But modern elites do not believe in authority. To them, all force is naked force, all use of power is brutality. All valor is stolen valor. In *The Last Jedi*, no one wins because no one deserves to win. In the nihilist worldview, there is no such thing as just deserts. Things just happen. Life is one pointless thing follow by another until death comes. It is far otherwise in *Star Wars*, where even the robot sidekick comedy relief characters are heroes, and have the moral authority of heroes.

Such is the foreground of this tale.

In the background is the Force, which gives moral stature to an otherwise light adventure yarn.

Nihilism says there is no truth, since all truths are relative. No truth means no hope. Star Wars says there is always hope, even if your father is a monster.

Nihilism says good and evil are merely different points of view. Nihilism says there are no absolutes, and that it is evil to speak as if there are. Only the Sith speak in absolutes.

Star Wars says life creates the Force that gives life meaning, and that evil is nothing but a corruption, a disease or a deprivation of life: a Dark Side.

The Jedi are not Taoists, and the light and dark are not equal and opposite forces. Despite how some have desperately tried to twist and misinterpret the few things in the film said about it, the original conception was clear: There is one Force, and it is bright. And the dark is an absence of light. It is quicker and lazier than the light side, so Yoda tells Luke.

In other words, the Dark Side is the get-rich-quick scheme that defrauds the chump. It is the shortcut, the easy way out. It is cutting corners. It is the philosophy that the ends justifies the means.

Such is the background of this tale. A poorer vehicle for carrying the modern message of nihilism cannot be imagined.

The second part of the same question is this: The film stinks as art and fails as entertainment. How well does it do as graffiti? As propaganda? Is this a female empowerment film?

Does it portray the agenda and worldview of the end-times feminists in a positive light?

I limit my comments to end-times feminism, the feminism as it is voiced and practiced now, in the last generation before the ugly philosophy is dismissed and forgotten forever.

Perhaps in the old days feminism stood for something like equality between sexes. Now, it stands for manhating, lesbianism, abortion, anti-motherhood, fornication, and witchcraft.

So, what happens when you take a character like Princess Leia, and try to make her into a feminist hobby horse? It simply does not work. One must either dismiss the feminism or change the character into her direct opposite: General Ruin rather than Princess Leia.

For a like reason, Luke Skywalker, the hope for whom *A New Hope* is named, cannot fit into the dark, cramped, smarmy, sick, verminous conceptions of political correctness. Political correctness allows for only two types of men: the innocent victim and the hated oppressor. There are no heroes in the Politically Correct universe.

But Luke is not a victim. He is a hero. One must either dismiss the nihilism or change the character into his direct opposite: Mopey Sulkwalker.

And, again, likewise for lovable rogue Han Solo. He cannot fit into a politically correct universe. He is more obdurate to character assassination than the other two, so the only thing that can be done with him is to assassinate him and shove his corpse off a bridge.

Again, there are only two brands of person in the politically correct universe. Neither one of them can fit into the Star Wars universe. The victim who needs a rescuer and the oppressor from whom the victim needs rescuing: and that is the whole roster of mankind. There are no rescuers in the politically correct worldview, because there are no heroes.

Belief in heroism, or even in its weaker cousin self-reliance, sinks political correctness at one blow. For this reason, the partisans of this worldview are desperate to smear, insult, denounce, and belittle heroism and tales of heroism.

Star Wars is a lighthearted heroic All-American space fairytale. When George Lucas first made the film, he was copying the mood and theme of *Buck Rogers* and *Flash Gordon*.

It is my belief that he, as a leftwinger in the 1970s, either did not know or did not care that he was also thereby copying the mood and spirit dominant in this nation in the 1930s and 1940s when those sci-fi space operas were made: a mood of a people confident and strong, mentally awake, and morally straight.

That 1940s mood is all-American. Luke, Leia, and Han have the can-do spirit that crushed the Nazis (which is, to judge by their uniforms, and what they call their troopers, precisely who the bad guys are).

The modern elite in Hollywood hates America, hates our flag, and blasphemes our God. Leftwingers in the 1970s had many years to go before political correctness would corrupt them, and turn them into Gollums, hating and fearing the sunlight, puking up the wholesome elfish waybread, and hissing and spitting at everything good and right. Star Wars was more good and more right than nearly any film ever made. It is wholesome, which, to them, tastes like dust and ashes.

In sum, they could not make Star Wars into a vehicle for manhatred, infanticide, lesbianism, and witchcraft.

They tried. All that happened is that the film-perpetrator made a film with the trademark Star Wars look and feel, but which morally and thematically is the opposite of Star Wars.

He peopled this shipwreck with unlikable, vile, and

stupid caricatures intended to be mockeries of our beloved heroes and heroines, and, for some reason, called by their names, and played by the same actor and actress, but really having nothing to do with them.

He made a so-called Star Wars film. It had the physical look of Star Wars, but the body had not one iota of the Star Wars spirit in it.

A body without a spirit is a corpse.

16

NO FUTURE

W hen someone possessed by the agenda of political correctness tells a story, he does not tell a story. He does not care about storytelling. What will be printed on the page or displayed on the screen is not a story; it is an agenda.

Star Wars, the most beloved, most famous, and most toyetic movie franchise in history, mother to countless shows, books, comics, games, and toys, ran afoul of the agenda: and *The Last Jedi* was the result.

What does this mean for the future of the franchise?

I can answer that in a sentence: there is no future.

Look at the snarled mess Rian Johnson has left for any future writer to try to undo.

Before *Force Awakens*, excitement was high. We were going to see our old beloved heroes and heroines again, and introduce a new generation of heroes. *Force Awakens* was not good, but it was at least as good as *Phantom Menace*.

True, it humiliated Han Solo, and turned his character arc in the first trilogy on its head. There, he grew from being a selfish rogue and a smuggler to a heroic lover, leader, father and family man. By stuffing him back into his smuggler role, they castrated him of all his hard earned gains: he became a boring loser, easily killed in one stroke by his emotionally disturbed son for no reason.

So Han Solo is dead, so there is no more drama or curiosity there, nothing interesting to see. He is not going to redeem his son in a reverse Darth Vader move, or get his broken family back together. Because he is dead.

Well, nonetheless, audiences were curious about Rey's parentage and Snoke's backstory. Where did he come from and how did he seduce Kylo to the Dark Side? How did Snoke get to be so powerful? Since the First Order is to the Empire as the KKK is to the Confederacy, or the Neonazis in Argentina are to the Third Reich, how and where did they acquire such vast resources, that they can launch a fleet overpowering that of a galaxy-wide Republic? And why did not the Republic build Death Stars of their own?

Instead of the coming-of-age story as happened to Luke, as he grew into his power after many a painful setback, we have the infinitely bland and boring sequence of a Mary Sue girl who needs no training, who is already expert at anything and everything, who cannot be tempted by the Dark Side, and who cannot change her wooden expression, for some reason wasting time on a planet where there is a crabby old ex-Jedi teacher with nothing to teach and no desire to teach, who, in fact, wants all the Jedi wiped out, and her along with them.

Then there is a scene where she is tempted by the Dark Side, except she's not, and a scene where she stands awkwardly and swings a sword around while sticking her butt out which I actually found painful to watch. I took a little fencing in college, and while I am no expert, I can tell a good stance from a slipshod one.

Suddenly she is better than the best Jedi who ever lived, and so powerful that Mopey is terrified of her. I don't know why he did not sneak in when she was sleeping to murder her in bed: that is apparently the new method of teaching this Jedi Master learned over the years. Kill the bad Jedi, and soon nothing but good ones will be left!

As it turns out, there is no room for character growth, because she is perfect. She has no family, they were drunk junk dealers who sold her into slavery for beer money. Except, if so, how in the world could she be unaware of the slave-driver to whom she was sold?

And why would she have been marking off the days, one by one, like a prisoner in solitary, if she had been raised a slave? What was she marking off the days until or since?

Would the slaver have simply never told her who sold her to him? How could she be unaware of the day she became free?

So the amazing revelation, for example, that she was Obi-Wan's long lost granddaughter, whose parents hid on the Sand Planet to save her life from Vader's Jedi-killing huntsmen, but who flew off to help the rebellion once they heard it had a new hope and a Jedi leading it... is never going to be revealed.

The amazing revelation that she is a clone of a dead Jedi Master who founded the Order a thousand generations ago is not possible.

The amazing revelation that her mother is still alive and needs help, or that her father is a Sith and needs redemption, the revelation of anything, anything, anything that might be dramatic or interesting is now impossible.

The amazing revelation that Rey is a Sith Lady, promised at birth to wed Snoke's son, Lord Dracolith, is now impossible.

It is simply not possible to come up with anything for this character to do, for there to be anyone she cares about, or to have any mysteries to solve. This movie dead-ended all those plot paths. They lead nowhere.

Even wrecked and ruined as Mopey Sulkwalker was at the end of this film, now that he is dead, there is no way for him to redeem himself. The master has nothing more to teach and nothing more to learn.

Yoda has turned from a wise old master into a cackling loon, except now it is not an act. He is actually senile, and committing an act of arson that endangers the life of his ex-pupil. What a moron.

Even dead, there is no story potential of any kind here. What can Yoda teach Mary Sue, professional perfect girl? She will end up teaching him. But since he is a loon arsonist rather than an impressive Jedi Master, it does not matter. Nothing matters.

Hotshot pilot has nowhere to go and nothing to do. He is a failed mutineer. He is not romantically involved with anyone, and he has no character flaws to overcome. You cannot do anything with a character whose sole personality trait is that he is a toxic male stereotype. He cannot even serve as comedy relief.

As for the alleged romance between Rose and Finn, do not make me puke. They have nothing in common, no screen chemistry, and no reason to develop anything in common. Indeed, Finn has every reason to hate Rose for her selfish obsession and her self-absorbed holier-than-thou attitude that made her ram her speeder into his, thus robbing him of a glorious death, betraying the base to its destruction, and almost killing him and herself in the process.

Toxic masculinity? What we have on display here is

toxic femininity. Rose is dangerous to herself, to Finn, and to everyone in the rebel base.

No matter what you think of women in combat in our world, no one in the Resistance should be willing to tolerate females as commanders or soldiers in any capacity, after the events in this film.

What plot is left?

At the end of *Empire Strikes Back*, we were excited: not knowing the fate of Han Solo who was kidnapped by the vile gangster Jabba the Hutt; not understanding the meaning of Luke's dreadful parentage; not seeing how the rebellion could succeed against so potent and evil a foe, we were eager to know and understand and see the hidden surprises promised in the sequel. The Emperor himself had not yet come onstage, save as a spooky hologram, remember.

There, the audience was burning with questions. It was a cliffhanger.

Here, what plot is left? What is there for anyone to be curious about?

Will Kylo switch to the Sunny Side?

Either he will or he won't. If he doesn't, there is no drama because there is no surprise, but at least that is consistent with his character. If he does, there is no drama because that would be inconsistent with his character, and one cannot wring drama from events that happen for no reason.

So, either way, there is nothing to be done with this character.

What about Princess Leia?

Well, the actress playing her has passed away, but even if she were alive, the character has nowhere to go and nothing to do. She has already blessed her son's death, so she is not going to win him back to the Sunny Side, or, if she does, we have the same problem that events happening for no reason hold no drama.

General Ruin has no rebels to lead, and no allies to reach. Perhaps Mary Sue can teach her how to use the Force, but why? She can already float through space, something no other Jedi can do.

If Snoke came back from the dead, or we found that Kylo had killed merely a clone or a hologram, that might be something to work with, but with him dead, the Empire is, let us face it, basically leaderless, and simply not a realistic threat to anyone.

Likewise, if Kylo was lying about Mary Sue's parents, and there is still some mystery and drama there, that could attempt to restart the stalled plotline, but it would at best be a make-shift do-over.

No one can write a sequel that will mean anything. Perhaps one could start over with all new characters, or have the time-tombs filled with Sith Lords long thought dead break out of their cosmic confinement, or set the next movie one hundred years in the future.

But who can stand even one more glance at these drooling idiots and this empty world?

No doubt the next film will be all about the stableboy with Jedi powers.

But it does not matter. Even if the next film is great, it will fail. Film ticket sales depend, for blockbusters of this size, on momentum, on buzz, and customer excitement.

There are three segments of an audience here: hardcore fans who dress in costume and show up in line a week before opening day toting toy lightsabers; casual fans who enjoy the films while they are watching them, but do not think about them after; and social justice warriors, socialists, feminists, lesbians, hysterics, lunatics, and witches who hate America, hate Star Wars, and rejoice to see ideals and heroes desecrated and trampled.

The hardcores are a base more loyal than any other audience for any other film franchise in all of human history. There are not that many fanboys dressed up in robes for the next Harry Potter movie, or getting in line a day early for the next James Bond flick. To alienate the Star Wars loyalist takes an heroic effort of unimaginable malice and stupidity. Yet Disney did it.

Now, I submit that most of the casuals are drawn to the theater because of the enthusiasm of the much smaller, but much more enthused, hardcores. They don't go on their own. They go because father or brother or boyfriend is a fanboy, or because they hear through the grapevine how many folk love the film. They won't go if the hardcore does not go, not in any numbers. Hence, if you lose the base, your tower falls down. That is why it is called 'the base'.

The casuals will not bring in enough ticket sales to pay the huge overhead of a big-budget special effects block-buster like *Star Wars Episode IX: Jedi Stableboy* is going to cost.

As for the lunatics and witches, they do not actually go to that many movies, they just pretend to be offended when movies are decent and normal and American, and they scream and boycott and bully.

Chasing them as a potential audience is something other industries, such as the comic book industry, have attempted to their lasting woe. The phrase "Get woke, go broke" has been coined to capture the folly of chasing social justice lunacy dollars. All social justice lunatics do is ruin. They don't buy.

Rian Johnson, it is clear, meant to kill the franchise. He

meant to tear down and burn up the past, and leave his mark on history as the man who desecrated the hope and light that Star Wars meant to so many fans. He is the man who singlehandedly dried up the Niagara Falls of customer dollars rushing to buy tie-in goods and merchandise.

Rian Johnson is Herostratus. Star Wars is his Temple of Artemis.

If that reference is too obscure, let me try again: *Last Jedi* is Room 101 and the fans are Winston Smith.

HAIL THE EMPIRE

L et us end with a song! My son and I composed the following ditty to be sung by the feckless stormtroopers of *Last Jedi*:

> *Hail, hail, the Empire!*
> *We will rule the stars!*
> *Our leaders are incompetent!*
> *But theirs are worse than ours!*

ABOUT THE AUTHOR

John C. Wright is a retired attorney, newspaperman and newspaper editor, who was only once on the lam and forced to hide from the police.

He is the author of some twenty two novels, including the critically acclaimed THE GOLDEN AGE, and COUNT TO A TRILLION. His novel SOMEWHITHER won the Dragon Award for Best Science Fiction Novel of 2016. He has also published numerous short stories and anthologies, including AWAKE IN THE NIGHT LAND and CITY BEYOND TIME, as well as nonfiction. He holds the record for the most Hugo Award nominations for a single year.

He presently works as a writer in Virginia, where he lives in fairytalelike happiness with his wife, the authoress L. Jagi Lamplighter, and their four children: Pingping, Orville, Wilbur, and Just Wright.

ABOUT THE PUBLISHER

Wisecraft Publishing specializes in stories of wonder. It is a supporter of the Superversive Literary Movement.

You can join our newsletter, A Light in the Darkness, here:

Http://eepurl.com/cg-4oH

WITHDRAWN

SAINT LOUIS UNIVERSITY

CPSIA information can be obtained
at www.ICGtesting.com
Printed in the USA
LVHW102020090922
728003LV00003B/402